Praise fo

"I feel so honored to be a small part of the Higgins' story as they initially began by training over 2,000 leaders using our ISOM Bible School program. Then they made the mistake of saying they "don't do orphans" and, as most missionaries know, whatever you say you "won't" do, that is very often what God will direct you to engage. With no missionary agency backing them and with the most meagre support coming from a Christmas mailing list, the sale of prisoner artwork and a host of other creative ideas, they built an incredibly impactful ministry that now, each year, reaches close to 800 kids through their Otino Waa Village and its associated ministries. In addition, they are involved in planting new churches and in helping thousands through their medical clinics. This book will keep you riveted from cover to cover. The stories are real and fascinating but they are also raw and honest. Bob takes you through valleys and defeats but also through many mountain top victories. I especially encourage the reading of this book by those middle aged folks who don't think they have much to give to the nations or to the communities around them. Think again. God qualifies and helps the faithful and the obedient.
    - *Dr. Berin Gilfillan, Founder, International School of Ministry*

"Bob tells this story with honesty, integrity and wit. As I read Bob's account of the founding and flourishing of Otino Waa Children's Village, I was again in awe of how God used their faithfulness and unique giftings to create a special place where hurting children could be healed by God's love. Bob and Carol left a legacy of love and excellence that continues to touch thousands of lives in Africa today. It has been an honor to know and be associated with Bob & Carol Higgins for more than twenty years as they made this God-led journey."
    - *Dwayne Friesen, Senior Advisor, Bend Research*

"This is an excellent and timely story, depicting selfless and heroic efforts by an ordinary couple who were thrust into an extraordinary situation."
    - *Andrew Seisky, former African Editor of the Associated Press*

"Bob and Carol Higgins are two of the most selfless people I have ever met. They uprooted themselves from their comfortable lives, devoting years to feeding, clothing, educating, and caring for orphans and widows a world away. Seeing how they helped children recover from trauma and find hope is humbling and inspiring."
    - *Sandy Cummings, Director, Lost & Found Documentary*

"As the Vice President and Assisting Director of Missions for our denomination, I visited leaders and orphan schools in many nations of the world. In my 22 trips to the continent of Africa, I believe that Otino Waa in northern Uganda is the best example of what can be accomplished in the lives of destitute orphans. Bob and Carol Higgins settled in a poverty stricken area ravaged by war, but were able to bring health and emotional healing to the many children they welcomed to Otino Waa. The Higgins developed a primary and then a secondary school that is now rated as one of the best in the country. I am glad to have witnessed this work from it's beginning to today when students have graduated and gone on to be leaders with many different careers and are leaders of their generation!"

- Dr. Clifford Hanes, former Vice President, International Church of the
Foursquare Gospel

"While this book is the story of one missionary couple, it's a model of Christian obedience and service for all of us. Bob and Carol's work required the obedience and service of their family and friends. Their work in Uganda became a team effort. With God in the lead, providing the resources along the way, they accomplished one task after another and held the people of northern Uganda in their hearts. The need to care for orphans and widows in their distress continues in East Africa, and the need can seem overwhelming. I pray this book encourages many readers to examine their own calling and, as Bob says, "do what you can, with what you have, where you are". With Bob's encouragement, I pray we can take up our cross daily and follow Jesus."

- Dave Shuping, Executive Director, PATH Ministries International

"Bob and Carol Higgins were retired school teachers who moved to Uganda to bring Bible training to rural pastors. They had no idea this would lead to rescuing orphans from a rebel army! Building a secure place for these children, along with food, education, clothes, and love transformed their lives. You will be facinated by Bob & Carol's riveting story of God's provision and hand of protection for them."

- Beverly Sallee Ophoff, Author of A Woman's Guide to Bootstrapping a
Business *and* Sunday Morning, A Step by Step Journey to Wholeness

WE DON'T DO

**The Story of
Otino Waa Children's Village
in Northern Uganda**

ORPHANS

BOB HIGGINS

~ with Mari Hanes ~

Published by Sure Marketing
365 NE Greenwood Ave #3
Bend, OR 97701 | https://sure.marketing

Sure Marketing maximizes the reach of churches and nonprofits, specializing in online promotion of Christian ministries.

Story Editor: Mari Hanes
Copyeditor: Jim Tucker
Cover Design & Formatting: Brent Earwicker

Printed Worldwide

ISBN 979-8-218-28101-4 (paperback)
ISBN 978-1-64508-320-7 (epub)

Dedicated to my wife, Carol.
She was engaged to the fullest
in every Ugandan endeavor.

CONTENTS

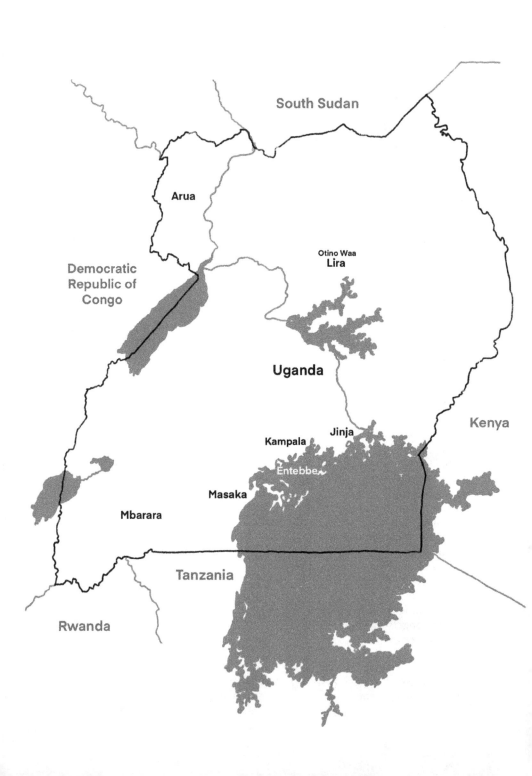

South Sudan

Arua

Democratic
Republic of
Congo

Otino Waa
Lira

Uganda

Kenya

Jinja
Kampala
Entebbe
Masaka

Mbarara

Tanzania

Rwanda

1997 — Bob & Carol Higgins' First Trip to Uganda

1998 — Second Trip to Uganda Introduced to ISOM

1999 — Moved to Uganda
ISOM Schools started in Uganda, Rwanda & Congo
All of our equipment is stolen

2002 — First Spring is Improved

2003 — Moved to Lira
First 10 Otino Waa houses are built to house 78 children.
Mobile Clinic is Formed

Ilera Community Church is Formed
USAID Grant Funds the Mobile Clinic for One Year

2004 — Primary School (Block One) is Built

2005 — "POP" Center is built with the first Hydraform Blocks
Circle Two Houses are Built

2006 — Otino Waa Cafe is Built

2007 — Circle Three is Built, the Bee Center Opens, Power is added to the property, & Radio ministry begins

2008 — The Town Office and a personal home for the directors is Constructed

2009 — School Block Two (Secondary School) is Built

2010 — Otino Waa Clinic Opens
Generator Installed
Circle Four is Built

2012 — Bob & Carol Move Back to Bend, Oregon

2013

>> Preface

Many people around the world are familiar with the name Idi Amin, the infamous dictator who seized power in Uganda in 1971 and ruled with brutality until 1979. In those years of political repression, ethnic persecution, and roaming death squads, it is estimated that between 200,000 and 400,000 Ugandans were killed.

Then, from 1986 into the late 1990s, Civil War raged in battles against the government by warlords like Joseph Kony, who led the Lord's Resistance Army (LRA). Kony operated mostly in the north of Uganda, and his hallmark was the massacre of innocent villagers and the kidnapping of teenagers and even younger children, forcing them to become child soldiers. In 1996, Kony and his men attacked a Catholic school in Aboke, a village near Lira, and kidnapped 139 school girls in one brazen act.

One generation had suffered from Idi Amin's brutality, and now the next generation was suffering from the brutality of Kony.

Bob & Carol Higgins preparing to live in Uganda, East Africa

In 2003, when my wife Carol and I arrived in Northern Uganda to lead medical outreaches and clean water projects, there was widespread destruction and displacement, the economy was struggling and political instability surrounded us. At the same time, the region was grappling with an urgent health crisis. HIV/AIDS was rampant. The disease not only decimated the adult population, but also left behind countless orphans, many of whom were fending for themselves in small villages, or in the bush. In 2003, the number of orphans in Northern Uganda was estimated to be in the tens of thousands. These children faced a bleak future, with limited access to education, healthcare, and basic necessities. In many cases, they were subjected to exploitation and abuse, and few places offered any hope.

Then one day, a local Ugandan Pastor introduced Carol and me to a small group of these destitute orphans, and we began to give them limited support, in the form of dried beans. But about one thing I was firm. "We don't do orphans," I said out loud and often. "We just can't do orphans. We have no resources, no network, or support. We can do a lot, but we just don't do orphans."

Well, this book is a story of what happened to the man who had made those firm and determined statements...

>> Chapter 1

HOW DID WE GET HERE?

"How in the world did I get here?" I wondered. I felt totally stranded.

I was standing on the roof of our Mitsubishi Pajero in the dark of night holding my cell phone in the air hoping for a bar or two of reception. My dear wife, Carol, sat praying in our stranded vehicle. We were in the middle of the deserted highway in the middle of Uganda in the middle of Africa. The dark road we were on wound for two hundred fifty miles from the capital of Kampala to the far north of Lira and the orphan children who were waiting for us.

We were out of fuel because the fuel attendant in Kampala had not cleared the pump to zero and I got far less fuel than what I paid for. There was no traffic, no AAA, and no town within walking distance. Not a single point of light from any house or hut. I was beyond agitated at being shorted on my fuel, more than a little spooked being stranded in the dark worried about our safety, and feeling quite helpless and isolated with no phone connection. "How did I get here?" I asked myself again.

But I knew the answer. It was because of the Big Question I had been asked years before.

The tops of cars work to find reception when there are no large anthills nearby.

The Big Question came as a surprise. We had no hint it was coming. It caught us off guard. There was something for us to think about that was beyond anything we had ever considered.

A little background will give some substance to our story. Carol and I were both teachers in central Oregon during our early married years. She was home economics and I was a shop teacher. When sons Thad and Matt came along, Carol quit teaching and I continued in the local middle school for several more years.

I left teaching to become a building contractor, some new construction, and more remodeling. After years of that, the opportunity arose for us to pastor the little church in the farming community of Alfalfa, near Bend. We started out on a self-imposed trial basis since pastoring was not our training or previous experience. We would try pastoring for three months and then reevaluate. Maybe it would work for us and for the church members, we would try it and see. Starting with six faithful members we did our best and three months turned into seven years. In the end, a robust Sunday would have been sixty in attendance. I wore my contractor hat four days a week and my pastor hat three days a week. What an experience!

During this time several pastors would meet weekly to talk and pray together and meet monthly with our wives for a meal. Friendship sprung from this fellowship, which brings me back to the opening comments.

The Big Question came from Nels and Laurie Church. Nels was one of the pastors from the group. "Would you go with us to Uganda and help put on a week-long pastors' conference?" "What? Go to Africa? I don't even know where Uganda is!" It was almost laughable to consider.

We held no longing to go to Africa. We had not been hoping for years for such an opportunity. We were quite content with our current life.

After talking this over with friends, family, and each other, we warmed to the idea enough to take it as a serious request. Details as to the cost and duration and what we needed to do gave us points to consider to determine if such a trip was even possible.

3

Our "highly unlikely" attitude was turning into reality as we sat aboard a very long flight from Redmond to Entebbe, Uganda in November 1997. There were several legs to that journey. Our route was from Redmond to Seattle to London to Entebbe.

This trip was filled with many firsts; our first trip to Africa, our first splash bath in an outside banana leaf stall, our first outside pit latrine toilet, our first time being in the minority in an all-black society, our first time being the richest person in sight, first time speaking with an interpreter.

The conference was held outside the town of Mbarara, three-plus hours from Kampala, and was led by Pastor Naboth. It was a success overall, but we did have some challenges. The heavy rain produced a lot of sticky mud, sticky mud clung to the pickup which was our transportation. Pushing the pickup through sticky mud left us a mess and delayed our start time. Oh well, Africa time!

Traveling to another country, especially one like Uganda, can expose you to microbes your body is not used to. Some of those microbes found us with dramatic results. I mentioned earlier the pit latrine. Being this kind of sick, walking a muddy trail to get there, encountering the offensive smell, the unaccustomed squat, and a cloud of flies makes your weak body fight collapse. This definitely was not a vacation in Paradise. Add to that the emergency dash to the latrine in the dark of night.

A few lines from Carol's journal:

> Wednesday about midnight I awoke to kerosene (from lanterns) making me very nauseated.
>
> I got up to vomiting and diarrhea. So weak it was a great effort to

4

get back to bed only to get up to more of the same.

Two nights, one day in bed has made a very sore back.

Carol recovering from the misery of village sickness.

But how could we complain? Many of the village pastors had to walk for miles to get there. At night they slept on a mat on the ground or on a wooden bench in the church. Not much comfort but they came anyway.

There was preaching and singing and praying. And, oh what singing and praying there was! We ate well. It was a good conference, mostly.

Before we headed home Carol and I were asked to return for the next year's conference. I really don't think it was our eloquent preaching or grasp of doctrinal truths that prompted the invitation. The heart of the matter was this. If we agreed to do the conference, we had to pay for it! That meant paying our own airfare and expenses for the Uganda trip as well as feeding about a hundred people for a week. There would be generator fuel to buy, some pastor transport to pay; fuel for the pickup, and kerosene for the lanterns. Somehow we were persuaded to say yes to the 1998 conference.

Trying to adjust the mud and mire to give the pickup a sliding chance at passage.

This was our introduction to Africa. We had flown the eight and a half hours to Europe and were only halfway there. We dragged our way through jet lag and lived in the village for a week of preaching and teaching and sickness and mud. We saw poverty up close, saw pastors eager to learn, and experienced their acceptance and love. There was a lot to think about on the long plane ride back to Bend, Oregon. Back to that place of family and familiarity and safety. But somehow, the people of Uganda had already worked their way into our hearts.

>> Chapter 2
WHAT IS ISOM?

The pastor of the church we were a part of back home in Bend had attended a conference where he saw an amazing presentation of a new video-based curriculum for training 3rd world church leaders. The video teacher spoke in English and interrupted his phrases and sentences with a long pause, to allow for interpretation. When taken to a non-English speaking country, a person who could speak English, and his native tongue, could hear the English and then speak his language into the pause, making it a bilingual presentation. It was a perfect format for Uganda!

Uganda had been a British colony for years, gaining its independence in 1962. English was the official language of the country, but at the village level, many traditional tribal languages were the norm. This curriculum was perfect for the Ugandan pastors who had attended the prior conference.

I contacted the ministry that had the video curriculum."Is there any way I could take a sample of the video curriculum to Uganda to try it out?" The answer was yes and we were set to take it. Arrangements were made for the church leaders who would be attending the conference to stay for a second week so we could introduce them to the curriculum. The video curriculum is titled International School of Ministry (ISOM).

In November, we flew back to Uganda, drove back to Mbarara, did the week of pastors' conference, and prepared to do a week of bilingual Bible School with ninety church leaders. We were equipped with a generator, an extension cord, a TV for a monitor, a tape deck, a microphone, and speakers. When lessons started some could understand the English, and others picked the Ankole from their Ugandan interpreter.

Once they had completed the first section of lessons they were facing a test. Many of them had only had a few years of school of any kind. The thought of taking a test was high drama! A point-by-point review readied them. True or false and multiple choice questions called for their answers. Papers were traded, answers read out, and scores marked. To their delight, most passed. There was dancing and shouting! They were relieved, excited, and thrilled, all at once! A fresh review and retesting brought most who had not passed to a passing grade. The training was marvelous. These village pastors never had such high-quality intensive Bible teaching! In just one week some asked, "Is there anything more to learn? I think we have learned it all."

This week of class gave us the foundation we needed. The teachers were excellent in content and delivery. The bilingual format worked for the mixed language group gathered there. They learned from it and passed a test. The gospel lessons touched them deeply. After only one week they went home with confidence they had a message to share that was accurate and true.

International School of Ministry gave all the students access through its bilingual format.

As we returned to the US our minds were churning. We were both trained as teachers so this was very familiar in format. We didn't have to teach all those lessons. We just needed to train a local lead pastor to set up equipment, find an interpreter, do review and testing, and send the results to the US office.

Our two sons were both married, our house was paid for, and we were in our mid-50s. There was a huge need for these rural pastors to get some training. As trained teachers, we felt we could do it.

"Carol, do we dare think of moving to Uganda to set up ISOM schools?" It seemed this was next in our life and we should at least try. "Was this God's calling for us?" Well, we did not have anything stronger than the feeling we should try to do it. We consulted with our sons and friends and received their hearty support. A few others were opposed. "Don't go!" After careful consideration the decision was made, and we were moving to Uganda.

There was a lot to do in preparation for this major life shift. I decided I was retired from regular work. We remodeled the attached woodshop and one bay of the carport into an apartment. That would give us a place to call home when we returned to the US each year. Son Thad and his family would be living in the main house.

Carol wrote a letter to our Christmas list telling them of our intended move and invited them to send gifts if they wanted to help train Ugandan pastors. We sold my red Mazda work pickup and camping trailer. We moved our stuff out of the house into the new apartment and into the storage area by the garage.

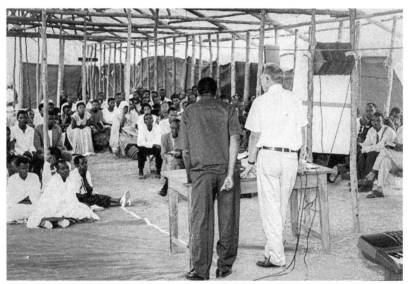

Teaching a session at the pastors' conference with an interpreter.

Passports, airline tickets, and four boxes of possessions is all we had as we headed out. Looking back, I would not say we were well-positioned for success. We were too old (fifty-five), had no mission training, had not worked with minority groups (now we were the minority), had not attended Bible school, and had meager funds in our account. Not even a sending church. We were very independent missionaries.

We knew the rural pastors had almost no Bible training. The need was evident. We had tried out the curriculum and it was quality teaching and would work well in Uganda. As former teachers, we knew we could make it work. This was about all we knew. But it was enough to give us direction, hope, and a pinch of confidence that this could work. How this would all play out – we had no idea.

"Not by might nor by power, but by My Spirit," says the Lord of hosts.
- Zecharaiah 4:6b

Leaving grandkids behind as we headed out to Africa tugged mightily at our hearts.

>> Chapter 3

WELL, THEY TOLD US NOT TO GO!

It was May of 1999 when British Air delivered us to Entebbe, Uganda. It was hard to believe, but we were moving to Uganda. We were greeted by Vincent and Godfrey, Ugandan friends, whom we had met on previous trips. They had found a house for us to rent in Kampala and took us there. It had running water, a flushing toilet, and power. All good. But it was totally empty; not a table, chair, bed, pot, or dish. So, they took us shopping to get at least a foam mattress to sleep on for the first night.

Without their help that first week, I don't know how we would have gotten settled. Godfrey had a pickup and devoted himself to us, taking us shopping for all our essentials and hauling them to our house. I was jangled by the noise, traffic, press of people, and total lack of anything familiar.

We brought US dollars in a money pouch under my shirt and in a secret pocket in Carol's skirt. To have spendable cash we exchanged dollars for Uganda Shillings at a Forex Bureau. Exchanging currencies left me a little dazed. I got 1,600 Shillings per dollar. So, if something cost 16,000 Shillings, that was $10. This made shopping very stressful for me as I tried to mentally divide the price of an item by 1,600 so I had some idea of the dollar cost. I relied heavily on Godfrey as we shopped to verify if the price I was paying was reasonable or inflated. Inflated because I was a white guy – therefore rich.

I realized that I felt very stressed in this new place. "Why is my stomach in a knot all the time?" There were several reasons my comfort zone had vanished.

We had no car. To get around everyone used the 'taxi" which was a Toyota minivan. They stuffed in fourteen people and off we went. Being new, I didn't know where to go to buy what I needed and was not sure even where the taxi was going!

After arriving, hopefully, someplace close to my destination, I wandered the streets searching for things on my list. Getting home, I hoped to get off close enough to walk and find the house. An example of this involves our printer. I had purchased a device in the US to plug into the 240v socket which was supposed to reduce the current to 110v. The printer, which I brought from the US, would be protected against high voltage. As I plugged it in, a layer of white smoke drifted out onto the table. Unknowingly, I had just fried the printer. Then I was wandering the streets in search of a shop that could repair my crispy printer.

And I was uncomfortable being a white guy in a black society. In the past, I had almost no interaction with minority groups. Now I was in the minority. I felt very self-conscious and uneasy walking around.

My feelings were all self-imposed for the people of Uganda were friendly, non-threatening, and accepting of me.

All the newness happening at once was my struggle. There was new currency, new prices, new transportation by taxi, new climate, new outdoor food markets, new culture, and new banking.

As months passed, more of life became familiar and comfortable. The more you do something the more normal it becomes. By the end of the year, my stomach was no longer in a knot.

Carol's struggles were not with all the newness. Her struggles were with leaving home, family, and grandkids behind. She longed to have them nearby. She even drew their faces as she longed to see them, feeling very sad at being separated from them.

It all came to a head one weekend I was away. She was all alone, sitting in one room and then another, praying in anguish. Seeking God to help her accept this African assignment and get over being deeply troubled. By the end of the weekend, she had arrived at a place of peace. God and Carol had worked it out and she was "mostly okay." Missing the grandkids as they grew up tugged at her heart throughout our years in Uganda. Missing graduations, birthdays, holidays, and baptisms, are celebrations you do not get to redo. They happened without you and you never get those moments back. That was the heavy cost of living in Uganda as foreign missionaries.

We soon learned the names of places, which taxi to take to get there, the prices of common items, and how to buy the food we needed. Fruit and veggies were from an open-air market, beef was carved from a hanging quarter covered with flies, and we had almost no canned or packaged food. Bottled water and Coke were safe to drink. We were learning how to operate in this brand-new place we called home.

One day on the way home we stopped at the outdoor market and bought a chicken. They grabbed a live chicken from the pen and soon handed Carol the ready-to-cook bird in a plastic bag. Having the warm chicken in her lap, on the taxi ride home was almost too much for her. Carol was thinking, "How can I cook and eat this chicken that was alive less than an hour ago?" If we hadn't grown up in the country we could never have managed!

We bought a wicker chair and loveseat with foam cushions to have a degree of comfort. The bed had slats, foam mattresses, and mosquito nets to keep out malaria-carrying mosquitoes. There was always a fan whirring to move the hot night air. Through the open windows, we heard music blaring, babies crying, and dogs' incessant barking. "Would we ever get some sleep?"

And there were other worries. We noticed while doing dishes that turning the water on and off gave us an electric shock! The wiring was seriously lacking for that to happen. So we became very careful to only touch the metal sink or faucet with a dry towel in hand.

The city water supply was unreliable so each house had a reserve water tank on a stand, elevated fifteen feet high. At night we noticed two metal members of the tank stand, which were close but not touching, had electricity arcing between them. You could hear it zap across the gap. Even with my limited electrical experience, I knew something was seriously wrong with the grounding. But the landlord was not worried or about to do anything about it. So we just learned not to grab on tight to any metal fixture, or it could be our last.

Our first furniture arriving with the help of our Ugandan friends.

The Ugandan landlord's thinking was, "If the lights in the house still come on, and the new American renters have survived the shocks, all is well." Our conclusion was quite different, at odds somehow. We were thinking, "We could die! Something is terribly wrong here! We are moving, very soon!"

This was some of our initial cultural education. Our American thinking was different from our African thinking. Different cultures see the same set of circumstances, evaluate what they see, and arrive at totally different conclusions.

WE DON'T DO ORPHANS

We were learning there were few codes, little or no enforcement or inspections, and maintenance only happened if complete failure rendered an item useless. This was the extreme version of, "If it isn't broken, don't fix it. "

So, learning to live in a new culture, which was very different from our life back home, was stretching us into new territory. This was just the beginning of many more lessons coming to us in the near future.

"Therefore, my beloved brothers and sisters, be firm, immovable, always excelling in the work of the Lord, knowing that your labor is not in vain in the Lord."
- 1 Corinthians 15:58

>> Chapter 4
THE JOY OF TRANSLATIONS

Jimmy O'Nalley had been our Ugandan interpreter for the week of ISOM school in Mbarara the previous year. He invited us to come to his hometown, as soon as we were settled in Kampala, to put on the school for the church leaders in his area. Mbarara and Arua were on opposite sides of Uganda and we had not yet traveled to Arua. The roads were bad and the bus there took eight hours. Heeding advice we loaded our equipment on a small Missionary Aviation Fellowship (MAF) plane and flew to Arua.

Our only means of communication with Jimmy was sending a fax from a nearby post office in Kampala to the post office in Arua. We then relied on Jimmy checking the fax logbook to see if any message had been sent to him. There were no landlines and no cell phones. As we flew we hoped he had received the message that we were coming since we had received no reply. Seeing Jimmy waiting for us at the small airstrip was a welcome sight. The next morning we met the twenty eager pastors and elders Jimmy had assembled!

The town had a generator so there was power during the day. At night it was switched off after eight. So we had the power to run the TV, which was our monitor, and for the VHS tape deck to play the lessons. Our first ISOM school was officially launched.

Jimmy interpreted the English into Lugbara so the bilingual presentation was understood by all present. Each lesson was about forty-five minutes long so five or six lessons a day were possible. This included breaks, reviews, and tests. Determined, best describes these students.

We were delighted to complete a week of school with them and then send them on their way to be in their churches on Sunday. We flew back to Kampala happy but exhausted.

Then we started an ISOM school in Mbarara with Pastor Naboth. Many of those pastors had attended the sample lessons from the year before so they were familiar with the lessons and how the school would run. This time they numbered about eighty.

For this school, we needed a generator, long extension cord, TV, VHS tape deck, microphone, and speakers. Our goal while spending the first week of school at each location was to train the pastor in charge to run all the equipment. Also to have several good interpreters ready to speak each day. They had to trade-off, it was a lot of talking and thinking in two languages. There was the clerical work of registration, recording grades, and collecting a small school fee to pay for their book. The pastor in charge of running the school had a lot of details to attend to.

Pastors came from miles around so food, water, temporary latrines, and bathing areas had to be provided. Generator fuel and kerosene for lamps at night were needed.

All of that was a lot of work and it took the host pastor's keen attention to all those details if he was to succeed the following month when they came for another week of school. And he needed to do it without us being there the second week.

Following the schedule of one week of school a month made it possible to complete the five sections of the curriculum in ten months. These rural pastors liked the schedule, it worked for them.

Each of the five sections of the study was accompanied by a book. The book had each lesson outline and included all scripture references used in the lesson. The book was a valuable resource for later reference and review. Sermons could easily be prepared by simply following the outline in the book.

Our challenge was only having the book in English. Each new school that was started needed an English book and the book was translated into the language of the area. The hunt was on for someone with computer typing skills, who read and spoke English, and who read and spoke the area language. In Arua, they needed the book in Lugbara and in Mbarara, it needed to be in Ankole.

My job was to edit each of these lessons written in a language I did not know. I could not read the words but I could compare each page to the outline of the English book. I checked to see if main point "A" had sub-points 1, 2, and 3. I could spot any missing out-line points. I noted any errors and brought the list of corrections to the typist.

I did the same with scripture references. First Corinthians 2:2 is recognizable in any language. I checked for any missing scriptures and if the chapter and verse numbers were correct. And there were numerous corrections for simple errors in outline and verse.

Pastors in rural Uganda studying for a test following an ISOM lesson.

Each book received this edit check before it was sent to Vincent, the printer. Once a school was started they needed a translated book. The pressure was on. Remember, the schedule was set for a week of school each month. To be ready with printed books meant a book needed to be translated, typed, edited, corrected, re-edited, printed, and delivered wherever the school was being conducted in Uganda. And the timeline to accomplish this was two months!

Soon an ISOM school was launched back in Kampala so trans-lating the Luganda book was added to the endeavor. So, a new translated book in three languages needed to be ready every two months.

I had small sticky notes on a wall calendar tracking the dates for each school. They were color-coded by location to keep me thinking straight.

I moved around Kampala constantly, checking on typing progress, delivering edit updates, and getting proofed copies to the printer. On more than one occasion they printed into the night to have books ready to get on the bus the next morning for a school starting that Monday. The print shop worked with great diligence to keep us on schedule.

The ISOM enrollees were amazed each month at all they were learning. Early lessons like Foundations of Faith and New Testament Survey grounded them in basic tenets of Christianity. Later lessons taught the requirements of an elder and church structure. Most of these church leaders had never received any training so each week's lessons filled their minds and hearts to overflowing. They needed time to digest all they had learned before the next month arrived.

They were being transformed from village pastors, having gleaned some knowledge through their limited reading skills, to pastors and elders grounded in the faith. Their new confidence showed in their body posture of heads up, stride, shoulders back, and overall demeanor. And now they could answer questions about God without being defensive. They were gaining a wide range of topics to preach with confidence and conviction.

It was during this time that I was introduced to Rev. Dickens. He was keenly interested in taking the ISOM training to his home area in Northern Uganda. He showed me a booklet he had made, even before meeting me, outlining some of his vision for his home area, titled "Rural Penetration Mission". The ISOM training fit his vision for training pastors throughout his region. I could not know then that this man would become my longtime partner/leader in the miracle of what the Lord would do in Northern Uganda. His vision reached into the future more than we imagined.

The ISOM teachers came from many church backgrounds and countries, they were some of the best. The church was being built up and strengthened as each month's training emboldened the area pastors. They were on fire!

"So faith comes by hearing, and hearing by the word of Christ."
-Romans 10:17

>> Chapter 5

MORE CHALLENGES

We had been living in Kampala for three months and were settled in our rental house. The essentials had been purchased, so we had a table, chairs, a bed, and a bit of food on the shelf. Two ISOM schools had been started and a limited number of taxi stops were becoming familiar. We were getting a familiar routine.

We arrived home from a school trip when our house boy, John, broke the news to us. Thieves had come to the house and had broken in, forcing the door with a bar. John was home at the time and was threatened with great harm if he resisted them. He was told to go to his room and not come out. He obeyed.

The thieves took our laptop, five tape players, and printer. They wiped us out. That was the equipment we needed to duplicate the VHS tapes for the ISOM lessons. We could not operate without those machines. We were sent reeling at this loss. Stopped in our tracks. We barely had a start and now we had nothing.

We contacted the nearby police post hoping they could recover our stolen property. They informed us that for them to come they needed gas money for their police car! And then they would need more for the forms to be filled out at the crime scene.

We barely had any money, so their request was impossible for us. And their needs sounded unending. We were frustrated with the police, demoralized by our loss, and very disappointed that none of the Ugandans had told us that locking the door wasn't enough, it needed to be chained!

Using a computer at an office, we let the ISOM office in California know that we were out of operation. There was no money to buy replacement equipment. Berin Gilfillan, the founder of ISOM, knew us and had faith in us. He announced he was sending enough money to replace all the equipment.

Such news left us speechless. He had no obligation to send us funds. Yet he did it. Our disaster had been rescued from ruin. We weren't finished after all. And we were very thankful that the thieves had not stolen the training tape master copies. When new equipment was purchased we could resume with little time lost.

That theft almost ended our ministry in Uganda before it hardly started. Berin bailed us out. Because he did, many schools were conducted in Uganda, Rwanda, and Congo. Our fragile beginning was almost doomed, but some generous timely help was our rescue. And we bought padlocks and chains for every exterior door.

>> Chapter 6

IS GOD REALLY OUR PROTECTOR?

We met Charles and Martha through a common friend. They lived in Masaka, about an hour away from us. It was a friendly relationship with only an occasional meeting. They were older than us, were from Texas, and were very talkative.

On a trip to Kampala, they stopped at the bank to withdraw some cash just before they headed home. It got dark before they reached home. In the dark, their driver was stopped and men suddenly appeared demanding their money. They must have been watching at the bank and followed them. They knew they had cash.

Martha had been sleeping and was startled awake by the intruders. They demanded the money and Martha refused to give it to them. Maybe it was her groggy mind not yet fully awake. She refused. Maybe part of it was her stubborn attitude. She would not give them the money.

They shot her point-blank. She died. They took the money. They fled. Never brought to justice.

Even though we were not close friends, this was shocking news. We knew Martha, and now she was dead. A missionary wife was gunned down for a bit of cash. A couple hundred dollars, maybe a thousand had cost her her life. The bandits took her life for such little money. They probably spent it in a week. The freshly spent cash was soon forgotten but Martha was dead forever.

Martha's death really shook Carol. Carol was a missionary wife like Martha. This could happen to her. This wasn't a movie plot, this was real life in Uganda. We knew we were always being watched as a potential target of a thief. We stood out, we were white, and therefore we were rich.

Carol rehearsed in her mind the promises of God's protection. "A thousand may fall at your right hand but it shall not come near to you." "God will cover you like a mother bird's feathers." "God is your refuge, stronghold, strong tower." Her troubled mind grappled with how could God's protection be reconciled with Martha being shot and killed? Was God protecting or not? Could his promises be trusted? Was she under His protection? If Martha was killed, and she served the Lord and loved the Lord, what would prevent the same end to her life? She was shaken.

For months Carol struggled with this. Martha's death was final. And yet God was supposed to be our protector. Carol knew God was real, Jesus really came to Earth, He was the Son of God, and He died for our sins to be forgiven. But her trust in God was shaken. A seemingly unresolvable contradiction existed. God the protector had not protected Martha, his child.

The Bible assures us that when we seek Him we'll find Him, ask and He will answer. God spoke to Carol's distressed heart through a Bible passage. Jesus was having breakfast with his disciples on the beach after He had risen from the tomb. Peter asked Jesus what would happen to John? Jesus responded, "What is that to you? You follow me."

These words were applied to Carol's distressed soul. It came to her about Martha's death as, "What is that to you?" I will take care of Martha and that whole situation and I will take care of you. Don't be troubled about Martha, I have it handled. I am still God so you continue to follow me. I am the God of Martha and Carol.

What a marvelous Divine transaction that was. That message permeated Carol through and through and she was at peace. From that time on she was okay. Her doubts were gone, her heart was at rest, and her confidence in God restored her peace.

This calls to mind that God's ways are higher than ours. God's sovereignty displayed to Carol's truly troubled heart did not explain the contradiction but did make it perfectly clear and acceptable. God's answer, God's resolution.

Carol had been in a tailspin for months. But then a few words from the Bible, applied by God, brought her to stability and renewed trust. We go from a little faith to a little more faith as we experience life. When we are highly troubled we can know with confidence that God is forever faithful.

"Jesus said to him, "If I want him to remain until I come, what is that to you? You follow Me!"
- John 21:22

Chapter 7

OUR FIRST GRADUATES

As the first three ISOM schools were conducting classes month-by-month, we were identifying what worked and what didn't. We were gaining valuable experience, which we needed. Interest in the training was high, and requests were coming in for us to start more schools.

The schedule of one week of school each month worked well for the rural pastors. But the cost of feeding all of them for a week was too costly for us. We reasoned that if they were at home they would eat. So, they should bring that basic food they would have eaten at home and it would get cooked at school. The pastors brought their portion of food and a cook was hired for cooking their combined portions of beans, maize, and rice. The system worked. They did need to bring their own plate and cup.

As a new school was being set up we needed a large pot for cooking.

A Ugandan pastor who was helping get everything ready for the start of school was given an assignment. "We need a big rice cooker." He headed out with purpose and confidence, knowing he could soon accomplish his task. In a day or two he showed up beaming. He knew we would be pleased. Standing next to him was a very large Ugandan woman. He had brought us "a big rice cooker." He had done his job exactly as he heard it. We looked at him and at her in stunned silence. We thought we had communicated simply and with clarity, but it was a total disconnect! Sometimes when you think you communicated clearly, you miss completely!

Another funny thing happened. We were conducting a school in Ibanda that was being led by Anthony, a Ugandan friend from the previous school in Mbarara. He had been extremely helpful in getting several schools started. We were staying in a house he had secured for the week, and we were sitting and chatting after supper. Carol was talking with Edith, Anthony's wife and the Ugandan cook. Carol was wearing pantyhose and saw an opportunity for some fun. As they talked she casually remarked, "Did you know that a Muzungu, (slang for white person) could take their skin off?" The cook had never been around white visitors and was very puzzled by the comment. Carol reached down to her calf, pinched the pantyhose, pulled it away from her leg, and let it snap back to her leg. The cook fell backward off of her chair in shock and astonishment. She was sure she had just witnessed an unbelievable truth about white people. We erupted in laughter. Uncontrollable. After some minutes Carol showed the cook the mystery of her removable skin.

Usually, the school was held at a rural church. So, there was no kitchen, no running water, no stove, no counter space. Someone had to oversee the whole food scene. There were supplies to buy like cooking oil, salt, matches, soap, and firewood. Cooking pots, big serving spoons, and jerry cans to haul water were all needed. It took a lot of work and attention to detail to feed a group of fifty for a week. All that food prep with no proper kitchen to work in. So nothing was convenient.

Each pastor was required to pay a small fee to offset the cost of the book he received. It was a struggle for them to pay their fee. If they sold a chicken, that would cover the cost. It took much urging to get them to pay up.

When a new school was in the planning stage, equipment was a critical issue. If none of the pastors could round up any equipment we had to loan it to them. The pastor heading up the school would come on the bus to Kampala just before the start date of the school. Then he headed back home on the bus with the Honda generator, extension cord, TV, speaker, microphone, tape player, and books for each student. When five or six schools were in progress, conducting classes on different weeks of the month, it was a real juggling act to keep the equipment properly placed. During the second and third years, the ISOM schools covered more territory each year. Nearly all regions of Uganda had a school or wanted one. Several schools in Rwanda were started. Two in Congo, one attempted in Tanzania and preparations for Ethiopia. Our time was spent starting new schools, translating and printing books, and bussing assorted equipment here and there.

After six months of riding a taxi, we bought a vehicle. It was a Mitsubishi Pajero, a medium-sized Bronco-looking vehicle. What a relief to have our own transportation. It was very reliable and had cargo space which we often needed.

When all ten months of school were completed there was high excitement for the upcoming graduation. Many of them had never graduated from any school. In fact, they would be the first ones in all their family to ever graduate.

We invited families to join the festivities. It was a joyous day for them to receive their beautiful diploma. Pictures were taken, and everyone wore their finest. Carol designed sashes and hired a tailor to make them. They were purple sashes with tassels to adorn around the neck and left and right to the waist. The mood was best described as jubilation!

Starting schools across the region consumed huge chunks of our time. While not traveling, I was very busy getting books typed in yet another language, editing, making corrections to the typist, final edits, then off to the printer. It was hectic, but it was not drudgery.

Heading to the graduation ceremony decked out in their ISOM sashes.

It was something completely new to me and the challenge of it was compelling.

An incident I vividly recall was a school in Rwanda that was scheduled to begin and we needed to be there to get it launched. The day we were to leave found us both sick. Someone had to go because we had the training tapes. Laying side by side on the bed we both felt awful. So we decided we would take our temperatures and the one with the highest temp got to stay home. I was slightly less feverish, so I had to go.

I located a driver and he drove me to the Rwanda border while I lay in the back seat feeling utterly miserable. The Pajero had a speed governor and it would ding when excessive speed set it off. I pleaded with the driver to keep our speed low enough to not set off the dings. In my sorry state, those dings were almost unbearable.

At the border, he caught a bus back to Kampala and I had to take the wheel and drive on for an hour or so. It didn't kill me, but there was a high misery factor. Somehow I made it through that week, which turned out to be a great time of inspiration and learning.

In 2003 our ministry focus was changing. We had been persuaded to take care of seventy-eight orphans in Northern Uganda which required buying land and building houses for them. To do this properly we had to move there.

A Congolese man, Ndjoli, who had been working closely with us agreed to take over the ISOM school program. That relieved me of those responsibilities so the transition could take place.

During the ISOM chapter of our life in Uganda, we had seen wonderful results. We translated five books into eight languages. Quite a feat when I couldn't read a word of it. The schools produced about 2,000 graduates from the three countries. The ISOM training continued, I just wasn't in charge of it any longer. The excellent training strengthened pastors and churches across the region. The gospel message had been planted in the hearts of new converts and seasoned Christians and the church was on the move refreshed, energized, strengthened, and equipped, as never before!

"Whatever your hand finds to do, do it with all your might..."
- Ecclesiastes 9:10

>> Chapter 8

MALARIA

When we moved to Uganda we didn't know much about malaria. For the first year, we took mefloquine, as an antimalarial, but quit taking it when we learned that long-term usage could have serious side effects. Lab rats developed eye lesions and liver damage when given that medicine long-term. So we decided if we got malaria we would just get treatment.

Malaria is transmitted to people when an infected female Anopheles mosquito gives a bite. This results in a bloodstream parasite which is dangerous for adults and especially bad for young children. One of our guard's young sons was sick but hoped he would get better on his own. That would save the cost of medicine. He died from a lack of easy-to-get malaria medicine.

Malaria was a serious sickness, not to be taken lightly. Symptoms included body aches, fever, headache, and chills. Left untreated it could lead to death in 24 hours.

Malaria deaths are concentrated in sub-Saharan Africa, accounting for over 90% of malaria deaths globally. Uganda, being in that region, has serious malaria incidence.

Carol's symptoms were mild at first. She didn't feel good. Some body aches, a bit of a headache, some fever. Then it got worse. The first medicine she took was ineffective and rapidly she became really sick.

Dr. Bea, a friend from our church small group, was called to help. He saw the seriousness of her condition and quickly got her hooked up with IV quinine. Quinine was the backup treatment when other treatments failed – reliable but harsh.

Then we waited for it to take hold. An adequate dose causes temporary deafness, which she experienced. She reported later that she was talking to her long-deceased grandmother, as though she was among those who had left this life. She was almost in the company of the departed, not the living.

Slowly, she started to recover. She had been brought back from being overwhelmed by the tiny parasite received from a mosquito bite.

After Carol recovered, she asked the doctor what he really thought of her condition when he saw her. During treatment, he gave assurances that she would be fine. But in reality, he admitted he thought she had a 50-50 chance of recovery. What a sobering thought! Without his swift action, and his expert knowledge, dear

Carol would have died.

If Carol had died there would have been very few ISOM schools, no improved springs, no mobile clinic, no Otino Waa, no Ilera Church. I would have left Uganda.

When we moved to Lira the risk of malaria was much greater. We were surrounded by swamps, perfect for breeding mosquitoes. We had learned to get tested when the slightest symptom appeared. When medication was taken early, malaria was less severe.

We averaged malaria once or twice a year for the ten years we lived in Lira. It usually wiped us out for a week with all-over aches, fever, chills, and feeling totally sick. But then we recovered and went back to work.

We always slept under a mosquito net. Before turning the lights out, and sitting in bed, we searched for any mosquito that had managed to get inside the net. Little blood-red smears appeared when we succeeded in smashing one with our pillow against the net.

We accepted malaria as a normal part of life. Took precautions, like the net. Got meds when we got sick. We weren't preoccupied thinking about it, or overly concerned. Yes, it was a major health issue for everyone in the region and we did everything we could with prevention and treatment to keep malaria in check. It really did make you feel very miserable and very sick, but we survived.

>> **Chapter 9**

MOBILE CLINIC

Carol always liked medical topics. She had a thick medical reference book to read up on topics when she had questions. She read articles and had a high interest in how the body worked. When we moved to Uganda that medical side of Carol went with her.

When we were in the countryside getting ISOM schools established, Carol noticed when someone showed up with a wound or sore that needed attention. She was always equipped with hydrogen peroxide and triple antibiotic ointment and Band-Aids. She would seek them out, clean up the affected area, and apply for basic medicine. When it was covered with a fresh bandage she would send them on their way. It wasn't much, but she did what she could.

As more months went by and more treatments were given, an idea was taking shape within Carol. She posed the question to me,

"What if we put together a mobile clinic, that would travel with us to the village areas where the ISOM schools are being conducted?" She was thinking that while the week of school went on, a week of the clinic could bring treatment to those at the school and to the whole surrounding area. Her creative mind was in overdrive.

On our next trip home to the US she talked out her idea with our friends Randy and Trudy who owned a hospice service. They were medical people and took an interest in her medical proposal. It wasn't immediate, but at a later meeting, they shared with us that they liked the idea. They were sending us back to Uganda with enough money to buy a van and equip it with basic supplies and medicines to start a mobile clinic.

Carol was ecstatic! Her lifelong love of the medical world, and the huge needs she saw in rural Uganda, was a dream turning into reality. Turning her dream and sufficient financing into a functional mobile clinic was a huge new project.

She had the heart for it and I was the planner. Neither of us was trained medical people so we needed to find those who were. There was so much to do. We needed to locate and buy a van; get a list of the needed supplies and medicine; find where to buy them; and find Ugandan medical personnel. We needed at minimum a doctor and a nurse.

Step by step it started coming together. Chipper, the grown son of a missionary, located a van for us. Doctor Schirazi, whom we knew from our church small group, referred us to his doctor brother whom we could hire. Joint Medical Service (JMS) was the wholesale medical supply connection we needed.

The van was equipped with plastic cabinets to hold and organize the medications and supplies. Patient treatment forms were printed. We purchased little envelopes for the meds showing the rising sun, high noon, or setting sun, to indicate the pill-taking time.

We were all set for our trial run of the first clinic day. Permission was granted for us to go to Watoto, a well-established orphanage outside of Kampala. Upon arrival, the nurse took blood pressure, and the doctor checked out his patients. The nurse at the van gave an envelope of Panadol for a headache or chloroquine and Fansidar for malaria. Our system was in place and it worked. In the process, I learned a lot. Like saying cipro and metronidazole. I was sounding more medical.

A tent served as the doctor's office and treatment room. As the mobile clinic held more one-day clinics in the village, we gained experience. Douglas was our super reliable driver/logistics man who made certain that our arrival was guaranteed and that we had all the needed supplies. Seating in the Pajero and van provided adequate seating for all the mobile clinic staff.

We met Rev. Dickens in conjunction with the ISOM schools. He had done the translation of the book into Luo for the schools in Northern Uganda. He was now working with us as we took the mobile clinic to several locations in Northern Uganda.

Carol and Rev. Dickens were a great triage team. Carol was not bashful about moving people around to get them in line for wounds, malaria, sick babies, and other one-of-a-kind medical conditions. She directed them. That is, she was really bossy, but with a smile. Rev. Dickens told them the same in Luo.

While gathered as a group waiting for treatment, Carol and Rev. Dickens often gave a health talk. To the malaria group, she stressed getting mosquito nets for their family. The intestinal worm group got a message about digging a pit latrine to improve their sanitation.

Hundreds are triaged behind the perimeter rope as meds are packaged for the already treated patients.

Word spread when the mobile clinic was coming and people came walking from every direction. Rural medical care was sparse and sporadic, so the news of a mobile clinic with real medicine and a trained doctor brought a crush of people. Under Carol's watchful eye and bossy demeanor, there was order and efficiency. Each staff member had a job and knew what to do, so there was little wasted effort.

At first, the medication given to the patients was free. We just gave it to them. We could see that these village people had almost no cash. Poverty was their lot. Almost immediately we were corrected by Rev. Dickens. He insisted that no medicine be given without payment. We were to charge a few cents. It was a small amount for us, but a lot for them to pay. He explained to us that free medicine would be seen by the patient to be worthless and would be discarded. So from then on, we held to the policy, even though many whined and pleaded, they had to pay.

As Americans, we felt guilty for squeezing these very poor villagers for their meager payment when we could afford to give it to them. But we learned our take on the situation was wrong. It was a cultural learning moment for us.

We succeeded in putting together a functional mobile clinic. Even though we were not trained medically, had never seen a mobile clinic, hired staff with no mobile clinic experience, and held health clinics in rural locations not knowing exactly how to do it– it worked! An idea, a dream, plus lots of planning and hard work had become a reality. Carol's dream now had wheels on the ground, tire tracks in the mud, and medicines that healed, in the hands of grateful villagers. The mobile clinic was ready for serious service. To God be the glory!

"...I was sick, and you visited Me....Truly I say to you, to the extent that you did it for one of the least of these brothers or sisters of Mine, you did it for me."
- Matthew 25:36, 40

Chapter 10

PROGRESS AND BETRAYAL

The mobile clinic functioned well on the days we went to the village. We were limited to a once or twice-a-week operation due to lack of funds. So we went out with the clinic as often as possible. The clinic fund regulated our activity.

A disaster relief organization based in the US heard of our mobile clinic and made contact with us. They wanted to hear how we did things and see our equipment. They sent a staff member to Uganda to check us out.

We looked good to them for several reasons. First, we had a system that worked. The clinics we had conducted had worked out the problems so it was a thought-out system with no glaring weaknesses. We were solidly functional.

Next, we were located in Northern Uganda and conducted clinics in the vicinity. They had their sights set on the large internally displaced camps (IDP) that had been formed by the Army to protect the citizens from the Lord's Resistance Army (LRA) rebel group. So geographically we suited them.

The largest factor in our favor was our registration in the country. We had our Non-Governmental Organization (NGO) papers in order so we could legally operate the mobile clinic. They were new to Uganda and needed a registered organization to partner with. If they officially teamed up with us, our registration would cover them and open the door for them to work freely in the country. So we gave them a perfect in.

What they had to offer us was funding. They had received a $500,000 grant from the US government. It would be administered through the Consulate arm of the US Embassy. Their grant would pay for all medicine and medical supplies. It would also pay the upkeep of four US medical volunteers on a monthly rotation to help man the mobile clinic.

The grant would also pay for all Ugandan clinic staff and workers. It was designed to cover all the costs for one year. After a year, a new grant could receive applications. It looked like a good fit for them and for us, so a formal agreement was signed and we became partners.

Medicines and supplies were purchased. People were hired to fill all the roles for a large medical outreach. Four tents were needed for the treatment rooms for the four medical volunteers rotating in each month. When everyone was assembled for a day of clinic in the IDP camp they numbered twenty-six. There were doctors, nurses, triage organizers, drivers, pharmacy staff, and logistics staff to keep it orderly and efficient. It took a minimum of four vehicles to get personnel and supplies to the clinic location.

The clinic locations were close to rebel activity so the clinic vehicles had a military escort, front and rear. Beefy vehicles with mounted machine guns escorted us. It was a precaution and we were glad we never drew fire.

Once the caravan arrived on location there was activity for everyone. All had an assigned task. They knew what to do. A perimeter rope was set between vehicles and trees, tents went up, triage signs hung from the rope, and the intake table was readied. In twenty minutes the first patients were getting their patient card filled out and treatment began.

One tent was equipped to do minor surgery and wound care. Patients with those issues were staged outside that tent. If a visiting doctor specialized in skin issues the triage directed those patients to him. A family medicine doc got patients with all sorts of ailments directed to his tent. A local nurse was paired with each US doctor so she could interpret for him. Without that, communication would have been futile.

When needed, a prescription was noted on the patient form. The final station for the patient was the pharmacy, operating out of the back of the van. It was well stocked with high-quality medicine but it was not free. The clinic was free, but not the medicine. Even though it only cost a few cents, many of them struggled to come up with a coin.

The clinic treated intestinal worms, malaria, malnourished babies, tropical skin ulcers, infected cuts, cough, urinary infections, and sexually transmitted diseases. Some conditions had to be referred to the regional hospital. Cataracts, TB, broken bones, and baby delivery had to be referred. Aches and pains received Panadol which only helped for a few days. Some were beyond much help. Advanced AIDS could cause a body-wide oozing scabby rash, truly cringe-worthy. Not much could be done for them.

Sometimes the American docs would consult together in amazement. In their combined years of medical practice, they had never seen some of the conditions they were encountering. Most patients received treatment, some were referred, and some were just going to die. The visiting doctors treated more patients during their month with the mobile clinic than at anytime in their career. They were never idle or bored.

Making the most of the time was important because by 4:30 the clinic had to repack and head home. It got dark at 7:00 and travel after dark was forbidden. It was potentially dangerous. Safety for all the clinic staff was of the highest importance. If anyone was harmed or abducted the clinic would be shut down forever.

On a normal clinic day, 500 patients were seen and treated. The intake table had their names recorded. This was not a guess, it was an actual headcount. By the time everything was loaded up and travel home was underway, everyone was tired. It took great effort from everyone to see that many patients. The mobile clinic went out five days each week so the tally each month was 10,000 patients treated. That number exceeded what the grant proposal had hoped for.

It was new for us to partner with a large US non-profit organization. They had obtained the grant so they were pretty much in control. They were a huge organization and we were barely a speck in comparison. Since they were very experienced I expected a smooth operation. Before long we found out differently.

The first two doctors to arrive treated us like we knew nothing. When we told them how much medicine and supplies we would need each day they scoffed. Our previous clinics gave us solid figures to go on so we were speaking from experience. They were only willing to buy half the amount we recommended. We weren't surprised when the month's supply they bought was gone in two weeks. Maybe we did know what we were talking about, but they never admitted it.

Each month, funds needed to be transferred from their US account to our account in Uganda. The amount to be sent was about the same each month. There were no surprises. The banking had to be done in Kampala which required a four or five-hour drive. And they knew when we would be traveling because we would be taking the previous team to the airport and picking up the new volunteers at arrivals. The timing was critical for dropping off, picking up, and getting funds so the clinic could operate with the new docs. And yet, for many months, they did not send the funds on time. We had to stay in Kampala until the money arrived or we would have no funds to operate the clinic. Their volunteers. from halfway around the world, would sit and do nothing until the money came. We found this very frustrating and unnecessary.

Toward the end of the one-year grant, I grew suspicious that the Ugandan accountant's balance was off when the monthly financial report was submitted. After spending many hours verifying receipts, it was conclusive. He had been embezzling funds by falsifying receipts. I took his laptop so he could not have access to any accounts and barred him from the office. Then to my astonishment, the US office would not let me fire him! What? Why would they do that? Perhaps it would reflect badly on their organization.

When they first talked to us, there were promises that when the grant ended we would be gifted clinic vehicles and medicines and supplies. We would be well equipped to carry on our mobile clinic without them.

But what actually happened was they kept all the vehicles, and all the meds, and hired away all our medical staff! They didn't even leave us an opened bottle of aspirin! We had nothing. Nothing about all this was illegal. No laws were broken. We felt used and then discarded when we were no longer needed. They had completed their own registration in Uganda so they no longer needed to partner with us.

It was an intense year of mobile clinic activity. The grant funded the treatment of over 120,000 villagers. Our system worked. And the experience taught me a lot. If a similar opportunity comes in the future, I will want more details in writing, have more say-so, and will react sooner and louder if things turn sour. Overall, we were truly thankful that thousands of hurting people had received quality treatment from highly trained doctors and nurses. There are many enduring memories.

Chapter 11

WE DON'T DO ORPHANS

When we were in Lira conducting an ISOM school, Rev. Dickens told us about a group of children in a remote village he wanted us to meet. We agreed to meet them and on the scheduled day drove to their location. We were surprised to be greeted by several district officials and about fifty young ragged children. We sat, introductions were made, and the children sang several songs for us.

These children were being cared for by Pastor David and his wife at a place they named Golgotha. Orphaned or abandoned because of the murderous activities of Joseph Kony and his LRA rebels, the children were barely surviving. Even though Pastor David was providing, their situation was grim. Food was so scarce that a meal seldom soothed their hunger. Some days there was no meal. They slept on a mat on the floor, about five per mat. One thin blanket for all five left the ones on the edges shivering. Their clothes were dirty, torn, tattered, hole-riddled rags.

That was our introduction to those struggling children. After the singing (they were smiling and pleasant), some conversation with the adults, and a look around the grounds, we prayed for God's continued protection and drove off. Looking back on that visit, I'm sure the district men hoped we would step in to help in some way. We left thinking, "That was interesting."

Carol greeting the gathered orphans for the first time.

We had no budget for helping them in any significant way, but we managed to leave enough money for Rev. Dickens to buy a small bag of beans for them. Every few weeks we were able to send a little money for more beans. It wasn't much, but it was of some help. This went on for several months.

We were having a meeting with several of our Ugandan leaders when one of them announced, "You know, the children at Golgotha look to you as their sponsor." My immediate thought was, "No! We are not their sponsor. We don't have the money or any way to take care of them." The most we had done was provide some beans at very sporadic intervals. We were not equipped to take on the role of orphan sponsor. I told Carol, "Carol, we don't do orphans!"

The meeting ended, but the idea lingered in Carol's compassionate heart. To her, they were so needy, so desperate, so in need of someone to step in and help. To me, they were a logistical nightmare. We had no money, no budget, no prospect of having money for orphan support. Orphans are a long-term commitment, once you say yes. By contrast, thinking of the springs we improved, when money came in, we gave the spring improvement team the go-ahead and they did it. That was it! But orphan care is different. Once they are in your care, you are responsible for everything. If money doesn't come in the orphans still need to be fed. They still need medical care. They need clothes and shoes. School fees need to be paid. Without some predictable income, orphan care was unrealistic, in my thinking.

Carol, the compassionate one, and Bob the administrator, were hashing it out, seeking answers. It boiled down to being a great idea that was impossible for us to do!

But then Carol fortified her argument by laying a scripture on me. James 1:27 "Pure and undefiled religion in the sight of our Lord and Father is this: to visit orphans and widows in their distress..." True religion is to take care of orphans. How was I to counter that verse? It is hard to argue against what God has to say!

At that point, I cautiously agreed to support those children. Carol and Chris Earwicker, who later became one of our board members, put their heads together and came up with a sponsorship program. A child could be sponsored for $25 a month. As people signed up to sponsor an orphan, it started to generate urgently needed cash flow.

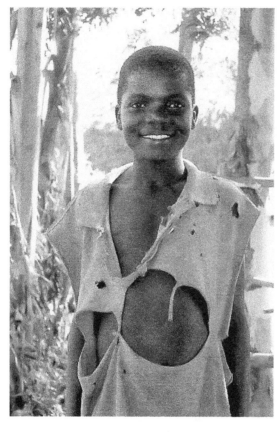

Gabriel in his "almost" shirt. They came with nearly nothing.

We determined how much food was needed each month and had it delivered to Golgotha. They were no longer starving.

The needs of the orphans tugged at the hearts of those who heard and funds came in. This giving allowed us to look for land to buy, so we could build housing for the orphans. Five parcels of land were considered before a selection was made.

Several factors were considered, as we reviewed each property:

1) It needed to be close enough to a town so we could easily buy supplies.

2) Have a good road connecting it to a town.

3) Be large enough to accommodate growth.

4) Be a usable building site, not too rocky or steep.

5) Secure from rebel activity.

6) Reasonable in price.

It took weeks of looking, to find a suitable property. We had our Ugandan staff do the looking and negotiating. If sellers saw our white faces, it made the price go up! Four neighbors, with adjoining properties, had a combined acreage of twenty acres. All of the owners had to agree to sell their piece so the combined property was large enough to meet our needs. Selling land was a clan decision, so it took a lot of talking to get everyone convinced to sell their parcel.

When the land was purchased we could start planning for the houses and kitchens that were needed.

On an earlier visit to Golgotha, we and the Earwicker family, took school supplies, basins, towels, and plates to the fifty children. We had been sending food each month for fifty. When we arrived, we found a group of one hundred twenty, not fifty. They had made the food for fifty and fed all of them.

Carol had been in contact with Pastor David and he assured her we should bring supplies for fifty. When we arrived and saw one hundred twenty she was highly agitated with Pastor David. (Highly agitated is a very diplomatic description of her mood.) Pastor David was doing his best to stretch his resources, but Carol saw it as being lied to many times over. Lying to Carol really pushed her buttons!

When calm returned, we assessed the situation and decided we would take responsibility for the eighty youngest children. Eighty was our limit. The forty older kids would have to make it without our help. It was a tough decision to make, but it had to be done. If too many are taken into the "lifeboat," it will sink. If it sinks, everyone drowns.

Bob holds his cardboard model for the first orphan homes.

The supplies we brought for fifty were divided up so everyone got something. It was doing what we could, with what we had, where we were. We were stretched to our limit. Really stretched!

Back home in Kampala, I drew a very simple house plan, which would hold four bunk beds, have a veranda for eating, and a room for a house mom. I even made a cardboard scale model, so everyone could visualize the houses to be built. Ten homes, each housing eight children, would provide a place for the eighty children we had just identified.

The land was purchased. The children were chosen. We were ready to choose the location for the first circle of ten houses for our new orphan project! Now, where on the property should we put the first circle homes?

>> Chapter 12
OTINO WAA BEGINNINGS

The ragged, underfed, barely surviving orphans of Golgotha were at risk of being abducted by the LRA rebels, and soon! Possibly that very night. Their fate would be child soldiers and concubines.

Within hours of being notified, we sent a truck and collected them for transport to Lira. Hasty arrangements were made with Lira Modern School to use three of their classrooms to house those first 78 orphans. (Two were missing in the hasty collection of those at Golgotha.) Rev. Dickens said there was absolutely no way we could go with them to collect those kids. It was way too dangerous. Besides, we had a lot to do to be ready to have a place for them to sleep in a few short hours.

We bought a mountain of four-inch foam mattresses and laid them out on the classroom floors so they had a place to sleep. By the time they arrived, it was dark. Headlights shining through doorways and windows illuminated the chaotic scene. It was a scramble, but they were safe, housed in the school at the edge of town.

The threat of abduction pushed our timetable severely. We were not ready for them. We did have land purchased and plans drawn for the first ten houses and the central kitchen. We planned to have the first circle of houses built and furnished by the start of the next school year, which gave us eight months. Now we needed to be ready in three months!

The orphans were temporarily safe from abduction at Lira Modern School.

They would be safely housed, would go to class, and the school cook would keep them fed. By the end of the 3-month school term, they would have to leave. The school would be in recess for a month and no food would be available. There would be no school supervision.

Our Ugandan staff rounded up Salva and Eskol, local builders experienced with brick and mortar. The brush was cleared from the building site and a center peg gave the starting point for a large circle inscribed on the ground. Ten houses placed in equal intervals around the circle gave adequate space for walkways and easy passage. An open-air kitchen was the central hub.

Truckloads of locally made burned bricks arrived and a swarm of masons appeared, armed with trowels and plum bob. The first bricks were laid for the footings and the buildings soon were going up with walls in place. Door and window frames were produced in Lira and were bricked in place as walls rose. Several houses were

Carol and I thrilled to see Circle One houses take shape day by day.

in stages of completion concurrently. The masons had a system that worked. Helpers carried bricks to keep those laying bricks constantly supplied. Some mixed mortar, some carried it, and walls went up.

Carpenters arrived to frame the roof when the walls were finished. Corrugated metal roofing kept out rain and shine. Progress was thrilling, but time was running out. Thank goodness two church teams came to help us put up the poles for the kitchen, lay plastic pipe for the simple water system, and paint doors and shutters. Everyone was busy with some part of the project.

Each house needed four wooden bunk beds, an eating table for eleven, two benches, a single bed, a desk, and a chair for the mother. All these had to be made by local woodworkers. Nothing was already made and ready to buy. Ten houses meant that we needed 40 bunk beds, made and ready, in the next three months!

Rev. Dickens, Douglas, and Carol were interviewing for ten widows to be hired as house mothers. Guards were needed, and a food purchaser. The girls' and boys' latrines needed to be dug (6' X 2' X 30') and enclosed. Four-room bathing enclosures were built for boys and girls. All that was necessary before the children arrived.

Cooking pots large enough to cook for ninety were purchased, as well as utensils for food preparation and serving. Each house needed to be supplied with bed sheets, blankets, mosquito nets, pillows, and a metal trunk for each child to hold their meager belongings. Each child required a plastic basin for bathing and clothes washing, a jerry can for fetching water, laundry soap, and hand soap. Plates, spoons, cups, toothbrushes, and paste were also needed for each child.

We didn't tell the children what would happen when the 3-month school term ended. They were unaware of all the construction. The day came and all were assembled for the news. They were informed they would be taken to a new place. With a house for them to live in and a bed to sleep in. A house mom would take care of them. They would be safe and fed.

It was more than they really understood. Most were young, six to eight years old. No one had ever slept in a bed, had a mosquito net, used a pillow, or expected three meals a day. Dazed, may best describe how they felt as they heard the news.

Otino Waa was the new home for the orphans now in our care.

They gathered their few belongings, loaded up, and off to their new home they went. Each child had a colored yarn tied around their wrist which corresponded to the colored yarn on the post of their house. So they knew which house was theirs, and the moms were there to greet them. This new place was more than they could ever imagine! The red paint on the floor was still sticky when they set foot in their new house. We were that close to not being ready for them.

It was a big day for us! All ten houses were complete. The kitchen was producing meals. Water flowed from the kitchen faucet, and from the faucets by each bathing station. Pit latrines and bathing areas were functional. The moms were taking their new arrivals into their care, helping them get settled, in all the new surroundings and unfamiliar settings.

WE DON'T DO ORPHANS

All the planning, hard work, long hours, and impossible schedule had somehow come together. The children were fed and in their beds, safe and needing sleep. Snatched from would-be abductors, they were now safe at Otino Waa Village; which, in Luo, means, "Our Children's Village." This new place was a safe haven for them to regain a childhood they had been missing. Without God's helping hand of favor, we would never have succeeded.

"Call upon Me on the day of trouble; I will rescue you, and you will honor Me."
- Psalm 51:15

>> Chapter 13
REVEREND DICKENS

We met Rev. Dickens Anyati Oyup within the first six months of our arrival in Uganda. We soon learned of his passion for sharing the gospel and his vision for meeting the physical needs of his Ankole people in Northern Uganda. He recognized the merits of the ISOM Bible curriculum and was instrumental in providing that powerful training to rural pastors throughout the region. We were a good fit!

As we traveled together, setting up ISOM schools, we later encountered the refugees in the internally displaced people (IDP) camps. These were seeking refuge from the marauding Joseph Kony (LRA) rebels. In an attempt to bring aid to those suffering, we put together a mobile medical clinic. Rev. Dickens played an integral part, speaking Luo, arranging for locations, finding personnel, and directing triage. To see and treat upwards of 500 people a day, with a staff of 26, required a lot of communication. Rev. Dickens was vital to the success of the clinics. We couldn't have done it without him.

The ministry of providing clean drinking water was another part of his vision for the region. Through his connections, and the help of donors in the US, over 250 springs were developed, providing clean water for thousands of people. Rev. Dickens also helped us locate and negotiate the purchase of the land for Otino Waa. Once built, he became the head administrator, responsible for staffing, orphan selection, and government interaction. He was in his home area, he knew the people, he knew the customs, and was a reliable, respected, local leader.

Rev. Dickens had a heart to serve his community, rescue desperate orphans, and honor God in all his doings.

The Ilera Church thrived because of his solid Bible-based preaching and teaching. His influence in the church world was felt throughout the region. This is but a brief summary of the areas of influence Rev. Dickens had. Ours was a relationship of mutual respect and appreciation. We met and talked frequently, addressing whatever issue was pressing us. No sharp disagreement ever marred our relationship. I valued Rev. Dickens as a co-worker in the Kingdom work we were endeavoring to do. We each had a role to fulfill and our combined effort moved us forward.

We also were blessed by the faith and wisdom of Rev. Dickens' wonderful wife Rose, who was as much a partner to him as Carol was to me.

It is not an exaggeration, to say that all our ministry accomplishments in Uganda would not have happened, without Rev. Dickens! God knit our lives together in unity and purpose. Rev. Dickens' unwavering love of God and people continue to bring healing and wholeness to a wide swath of Northern Uganda. I am thankful to God for putting such a man in my life.

"His master said to him, "Well done, good and faithful slave. You were faithful with a few things, I will put you in charge of many things; enter the joy of your master."
- Matthew 25:21

>> Chapter 14

FROM TRAGEDY TO TRIUMPH

Otino Waa had its beginnings tragically linked to the LRA rebel activity in Northern Uganda. Most of the first children came to us as war orphans. Some had been among those abducted and had managed to escape.

The horrific events they had observed or had been forced to participate in produced deep-seated trauma. There were scenes in their recent memory of brothers or sisters being killed, a baby in a sack beaten against a tree, an uncle killed by machete, friends drowned, or girls raped. They were faced with killing or being killed, perhaps even forced to kill a family member.

The mention of such horror is hard to believe or imagine. But, even at their tender young ages, they had seen it. They were right there. Some had been forced to do unspeakable deeds themselves or die.

Maybe, that is why Bella didn't speak to anyone for three years. We couldn't get a word out of her. But Auntie Carol loved on her the whole ten years they were together. So shy, Bella would stand close to Carol, waiting to be drawn in for a warm prolonged hug she knew was coming. Carol always told her how beautiful she was, how special, how loved. Eventually, she did speak, some.

Patricia was plagued with nightmares from what she had experienced. She had been abducted, escaped, and abducted again. Eventually, she found her way to Otino Waa and safety. Her trauma went beyond what any ordinary person could ever imagine.

Freedom and deliverance from her past came from God. She learned at church, and from age mates that experienced similar horrors, that forgiveness was possible, because Jesus died for all sin, even terrible sin.

This truth soothed the anguish that tormented her nightly slumber. Oh, what a relief to sleep all night, uninterrupted by a pounding heart and sweat-drenched body, reeling from the terror. The Savior died for her sin and it was real! It was real enough to stop the nightmares.

Jeffrey was deeply troubled. He had a hard time following the simple rules of Otino Waa. He would skip class, had a surly attitude, and didn't get along well with others.

His story involved abduction, blood, the death of family members, and harsh treatment. Gruesome things a young boy should never endure.

Some of his healing came from growing his own small garden. He did it well and it was therapy for him. One day, he presented Carol with a gift of a small bag of peanuts he had grown. Knowing the backstory, made those peanuts one of the most treasured gifts she ever received.

One day, Carol was sitting in her office mulling over all the things the Otino Waa kids were dealing with. Things completely outside our realm of experience. As she pondered, the thoughts came to her in perfect order. She took pen and paper and started writing. Phrase followed phrase, thought on thought. From start to finish, it just flowed smoothly from her pen. When she finished, it was done. There were no revisions or corrections. As she wrote, there were no hesitations or trying to come up with the next idea. She felt she had just had a God-inspired episode. She had composed, in a few minutes, the Otino Waa Creed.

She introduced it to the children and within a few days we were greeted with a presentation from a group of them – they recited the Creed in unison from memory. It took us by surprise and caught us off guard. What a pleasant surprise!

It so resonated with them that they practiced and memorized all of it, start to finish. It touched the core of so much of what they were experiencing.

That was just the beginning. Soon, each house was able to recite the Creed. At the weekly kids' meeting, it would be recited by a chosen house. Even the youngest, six-year-olds, were getting it, with the help of the older kids.

It was their Creed. No one else had a Creed like that. It summarized their life, at least in part, addressing their hurt, their sorrow, and their faith that God was their answer. A few words expressed so much that was true in their life. The words were a reminder, "Life is hard, but God is good!"

The trauma they felt was gripping and real. The Creed acknowledged their trauma and helped them find a way through it, relying on God. It was amazing to see their shattered lives mended and healed. They came as emotional wrecks and became self-confident young adults, ready to take on the next challenge.

The "Mamas" brought stability to each new home

The Creed played a part in their healing. If asked, I believe many of them could recite it today, probably with gusto!

"...Allow the children to come to Me; do not forbid them, for the kingdom of God belongs to such as these."
- Mark 10:14

Otino Waa Creed

I am a special child of God,
Chosen and saved for a unique purpose.

My life has been difficult,
but God has been and will be with me.

I have my own Guardian Angel who watches over me.

It is not my fault my parents are dead;
I will miss them until the day I die.

I choose to forgive the people and circumstances surrounding
their death because I know
my own healing and well-being begin in forgiveness.

In the future, whenever I feel sad or angry,
I will find someone who loves me and tell him how I feel.

I know I can always talk to God in my heart.

No one can take God's love for me away.

I am learning to be grateful for my life, knowing that God will
use me to help others who also have a difficult life.

Life is hard, but God is good!

>> Chapter 15

SPECIAL MEDICAL ATTENTION

When we lived in Kampala we attended a large downtown church, Kampala Pentecostal Church (KPC). We joined a small group that catered to expats. It was there that we met Dr. Shirazi. He trained in Europe as an orthopedic surgeon. After years of doctoring in other places, he returned to his home country of Uganda. He became our go-to doctor for many surgeries for our Otino Waa kids.

Joshua was one of the original boys at Otino Waa and it was evident he had a short leg. About five inches! Dr. Shirazi thought he could be helped so we sent him to Kampala for surgery.

Two cages were screwed to his femur. Threaded rods connected the cages so that by advancing the nuts on the rods the cages could be slowly moved apart. His femur was cut completely through but the cages held his leg firmly in position. As the cut bone surfaces began to heal, new bone was being deposited at the cut. Little by little, moving the adjusting nuts kept tension pulling his bone apart, so new bone kept filling the gap. This was causing his leg to grow longer. This worked but less than an inch could be gained. So Joshua still needed a custom-made built-up shoe for a balanced gait.

Jasper was a young boy who was hiding in the bush at night to avoid being captured by the LRA. If captured he would be forced into the role of being a child soldier. While in hiding an adder bit him on the foot.

When he came to us at the mobile clinic in the IDP camp, his foot was a mess. It had been way too long without treatment. His foot was black and useless from the venom and infection; the local doctors could only fix it by amputation. Dr. Shirazi said to bring him to Kampala so he could at least try to save his foot.

The operation involved removing all the bones and bad flesh from the top of his foot, almost to the sole of his foot. There was just a big empty hole that used to be a foot. I couldn't imagine that surgical wound ever closing. But with frequent clean dressings, over many weeks, that foot, though quite deformed, did heal. That wonderful surgery saved Jasper from a lifetime of walking on one foot aided by a walking stick. A few years later, he was wearing shoes and playing soccer!

Jimmy was a very young boy that came to us with club feet. His feet were turned so badly that the sun actually shone on his soles! When Carol asked him if he would like his feet fixed, he nodded yes.

Off to the surgeons in Kampala, he went. It was a difficult surgery to get his feet turned under so he could walk properly, but they did it. What a transformation. He went from walking on his ankles to making footprints with both feet! He could walk properly.

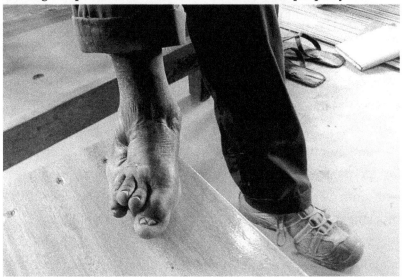

Jasper's snake bitten foot did heal after his surgery. It is misshapen, but he has a foot to walk on.

Oscar was born with no lower lip on the right side of his mouth. Hence, the saliva flowed unhindered onto his shirt. He was always an unsightly mess. No one wanted him because of it.

Carol's compassion went out to him and she became Oscar's self-appointed advocate. A grandfather was taking care of Oscar. When Carol sought his permission to take Oscar into Otino Waa, he quickly agreed.

Oscar was admitted as a vulnerable child needing special care, not as an orphan. It took considerable searching but eventually, a plastic surgeon was found in Kampala. And Oscar was accepted as a patient.

Several surgeries over several years were necessary to build up his lip and reform his mouth. But they were able to give him a leak-proof mouth that looked very acceptable. In reality, they gave him life. He was no longer a shunned outcast but a normal kid. He is now a young adult using that functioning mouth to proclaim the goodness of God– a true herald!

We came across Thomas while conducting a clinic at an IDP camp outside of Lira. As the mobile clinic was providing medical treatment for the camp, we saw Thomas wandering around the site. Through an interpreter, we learned his story. A local "witch doctor", perhaps just an elder trying to help, attempted to remove a bad tooth with a sharpened bicycle spoke. This explained the shocking plight of young Thomas. (About ten years old.)

His jaw was swollen about fist-sized and puss dripped from it onto his shirt. In the sun it dried out and became crusty. He stunk with the stench of infection. Carol said, "We have to help him!" I wanted to run! She prevailed and soon Thomas was sent to Dr. Shirazi.

He reported that the jawbone was so degraded that layers of it peeled away like layers of an onion. The surgery successfully removed the affected jaw bone and the infection. Then Thomas was sent back to us to heal.

The infection was so severe that Thomas would have died without the surgery. But he lived! And years later, as a secondary student, he was second in his class academically. He just needed someone to intervene (Auntie Carol), a skilled surgeon (Dr. Shirazi), and caring donors (USA sponsors), all lending a helping hand in his hour of need.

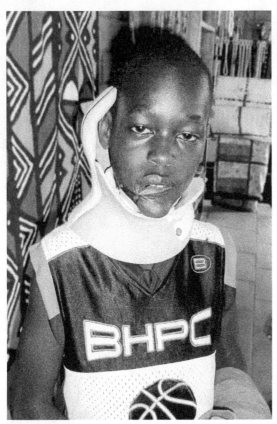

The plastic surgeons were able to build a lower lip for Oscar. Several operations were required.

These five stories are examples of the more intense medical conditions we were faced with. We didn't always know what to do. There were many successes and some failures. Like the baby that died while we were taking it to the Lira Hospital. We tried to help but unsuccessfully.

Carol and I were not medical people. But at times we were thrust into the midst of a medical situation that needed action, so with God's help we did what we could.

"But a Samaritan who was on a journey came upon him; and when he saw him, he felt compassion, and came to him and bandaged

up his wounds, pouring oil and wine on them; and he put him on his own animal, and brought him to an inn and took care of him."

- Luke 10:33-34

>> Chapter 16
OTINO WAA WATER

When the twenty acres were purchased for Otino Waa, a location was staked out for Circle One. Starting from scratch meant we had to plan for everything to make a community functional. As the ten houses, kitchens, latrines, and bathing enclosures were being built, attention was also being given to the water system.

On the high side of Circle One, the masons constructed a brick platform four feet high with steps leading to the top. A one thousand-liter water tank (250-gallon) was placed on the platform, able to gravity feed water to all points of Circle One. Plastic pipe from the tank brought water to faucets between every two houses and to the kitchen. Plumbing was done, now water was needed.

The first water came from a close by spring. Each of the original orphans was supplied with a jerry can; a small one for small kids; larger one for the older ones. Everyone walked to the spring and returned with a full jerry can. They emptied it into the tank on the platform. The moment had arrived to see if the system would really work.

Rev. Dickens opened the first faucet and what joy to see water come forth! It seemed miraculous, to those of a village mentality. They had never experienced running water in the village. We were instantly considered high-tech. We had running water in our village setting. The only ones, only us!

Before many weeks passed, we were able to have a well drilled on the property. It seemed like the Lord had smiled down on us when the best location to drill was the high corner of the whole property. That meant with future development there would be gravity flow to all points of the project.

A hand pump installed on the well made water closer than the spring, but it was still some distance from Circle One. Patrick, a man from the community, was hired to keep the tank full. He filled 5-gallon jerry cans, strapped them to a bike, and walked the load to the water tank. With 90+ people using the water, there was never enough. Constant arranging to not waste water wore us out, without much change.

Finally, a solution came to mind. A water flow restrictor could be made to fit inside each faucet. The water faucets had a shoulder just inside, before the adjusting valve. A plastic disc was cut from a discarded plate, just fitting against the shoulder. Candle wax in the sun was soft enough to seal the disc to the faucet. The smallest drill bit put a hole in the center of the disc which restricted the flow to a dribble. It was enough to wash hands, hygiene was accomplished, and water was conserved. This solved always being out of water.

For bathing, each child had to go to the pump and fill their container, which they used for a splash bath from their basin. They could use as much or as little water as they chose, it was up to them, and we did not care. Having to carry their own water was self-limiting. Washing clothes was the same.

The next water system improvement came through the US Embassy. They connected us to a company that had shipped four solar-powered systems to Uganda. They were unused, sitting in a warehouse. The company agreed to donate one solar-powered water pump to us since we were an orphan project. It replaced the hand pump.

The solar powered pump filled the tank on the stand which gravity fed water to all of Otino Waa.

The masons constructed a platform about five feet high, adjacent to the well, on which a 10,000-liter water tank (2,500 gallons) was placed. That tank was connected to the Circle One tank with a two-inch plastic main line. The Circle One tank was equipped with a float valve to turn off the flow when it was full. This reduced water supply problems to a minimum. There was running water for hygiene and cooking. We were becoming a model for water development!

The final step in our water system development came when an electric transformer was installed on our property providing grid power. The solar pump was replaced with a submersible pump on grid power. It could pump to fill the tanks all night if needed. When Circles Two, Three, and Four were added, the system was adequate to bring a constant flow of water to all the houses.

Water demand increased with the addition of the cafe, medical clinic, science labs, office, and many more children. The water system, as it transitioned from hand-carried water to an electric submersible pump, kept pace with the increasing demand for clean pure water. Essential water, flowing throughout, what a blessing!

"And whoever in the name of a disciple gives to one of these little ones even a cup of cold water to drink, truly I say to you, he shall not lose his reward." - Matthew 10:42

>> Chapter 17
SCHOOL BLOCK ONE

School would begin within a few weeks of the first orphans arriving at Otino Waa. The closest government school was within walking distance, about half a mile. So, we needed to get our first 78 kids enrolled. Being that close, made it the obvious choice. So off they went, walking along the side of the highway, to their new school.

We provided each with a few pencils or pens and a pad of paper. Very basic, but it was a start. They were placed in class by age or by earlier school experience. Most of them had very little school exposure. Their skills were rudimentary. At least they were in class!

We soon learned what little resources the school had to work with. It had nine classrooms, but almost no desks or benches. Children were mostly sitting on the floor. Each classroom had a chalkboard for the teacher to write notes on, which the students were to copy. Textbooks were not available, so the teacher, with a piece of chalk, was the sole source of instruction.

Fifteen hundred students were jammed into the nine classrooms. Most of the Otino Waa kids were young and unschooled. Learning to read and count and write is what they needed. The teachers were given a nearly impossible task, having no texts, no readers, and well over one hundred in each classroom. Trying to teach someone to read, under those conditions, produced non-achievers. Mission Impossible! The government had promised free primary education for all children. They were trying, but the results were dismal. It didn't help teacher morale when they didn't get paid on time, or sometimes only half.

It was soon obvious that we needed to build a school of our own, so our kids, at least had a chance to learn. To the drawing board, I went, to design a suitable school.

The school building had six classrooms each, of sufficient size to accommodate tables and benches for thirty students, plus a teacher's desk. All rooms had doorways that opened onto the covered veranda. The hip roof would shed rain on all sides and protect the exterior walls. Exterior walls were dominated by tall windows, to let in maximum light. Checking over the final drawings settled my mind, the plan would work.

My father was a major contributor to our first school building. He had been a teacher his whole life, so giving to a school was dear to his heart. When his and others' funds arrived, we gave Salva and his team of masons the set of plans and the go-ahead to start.

This, by far, was the largest building we had undertaken, 5520 square feet. The walls were built using blocks of compressed soil, sand, and cement made with our own Hydraform machine.

Metal doors and door frames, metal window frames, louver glass and window hardware, and then large welded angle iron roof trusses, were purchased or fabricated on-site. Brick arches connected the columns at the outer edge of the veranda. The 2" X 3" wood purlins were coated with used motor oil to discourage hungry termites. The purlins attached perpendicular to the trusses, giving a nailing surface for the Papyrus mats, (which cut the radiant heat), and then the final roof of corrugated iron sheets was screwed in place. The building was ready.

An African dance was being performed for a school program as seen through the school building arch.

Hiring teachers was now the top priority. Our educational philosophy was quite simple. We would hire the most qualified teachers available, limit class size to thirty, and have textbooks for every student in every subject. To start this process we aired radio spots advertising the teaching positions we had open. Written applications were shortlisted, and posted at the office, and those came in for an interview. Selections were made and teachers were hired. The same steps led to selecting the headmaster (principal).

Getting textbooks for all grades in all subjects was not quick, easy, or cheap. But when school commenced our persistence paid off, with at least limited texts in most subjects.

Taking these three simple steps was a huge improvement in the educational prospects for our students. Good teachers, reasonable class sizes, and textbooks for each student provided a greater opportunity to learn and advance. And it worked!

Within a few short years, our students scored the highest of all the schools in the Kole district. These orphans who had nothing, when given a chance, had risen to the top. We had not done anything brilliant. We just gave them a good, basic education and watched them rise to their potential.

School Block One provided six classrooms for primary students.

As would be expected, not everyone was a top student. Some excelled and some struggled. But they all learned to the level of their ability. Otino Waa Primary School gave us control over the education of our kids, which was an immeasurable benefit for those first classes and all that followed in later years.

Getting to go to school was a great privilege for our Otino Waa kids. Notice they have desks, chairs, and books!

"Make your ear attentive to wisdom; incline your heart to under-standing."

- Proverbs 2:2

>> Chapter 18

OTINO WAA POWER

Circle One was completed and the houses were filled with the first 78 orphans. The flow of life was taking on a predictable routine of meals, bathing, and bedtime. But it was evident that we would be greatly benefited if we had electrical power.

As I mentioned earlier, the first electric power for Otino Waa came through a contact at the US Embassy that resulted in solar panels for our well pump.

The solar panels were installed on the school roof and bolted through the roof with the nuts on the underside of the roof. This ensured no theft of the panels since a wrench would be needed inside and out. The panels were wired to the pump and sunshine set the pump to pumping. Soon the water was flowing to the Circle One water system. The solar-powered pump gave us an automatic water supply that transformed our water situation. It gave a nearly constant supply of water, it was wonderful!

Just across the highway from Otino Waa were high-voltage power lines. Power was that close to us, but remained out of our reach. Transformers were needed to step it down for our household use. Four power poles would have to be placed and transformers installed on our side of the road. If we were to get power, we would have to pay the power company for the installation, and then pay our monthly power bill. I had feelings this arrangement was a bit of a rip-off. Besides, we lacked the funds to make it happen.

One day Dale Russell, our US Operations Manager, bumped into a friend while shopping. As they talked, Dale shared the power situation at Otino Waa and the huge benefits power would bring to all parts of Otino Waa. That conversation resonated with Dale's friend and resulted in the project being completely funded. All, from a "chance" meeting in the grocery store.

Having funds available set the project in motion. Soon, power poles were set and transformers were installed. We had access to grid power.

We immediately called Joseph, an experienced electrician friend. He made a list of electrical equipment and parts and supplies needed. Funds were available for the initial wiring to begin. Ditches were dug to bury the wire, and no overhead lines were used. Surface-mounted conduit brought wires to switches, plugs, and lights in the buildings. There was joy and amazement when the switch was flipped and darkness was eliminated!

Electric power created opportunities never before open to us.

Computers and phones could be powered and charged, illumined rooms meant darkness did not stop the activity. Exterior lights were a game-changer for security. Power tools could be used for construction. Lights at the front gate were the only ones shining along that stretch of highway. Grid power set us apart. We were obviously a very advanced place. We had power!

Excitement was high as our dreamed-of transformer became a reality.

Solar power was a great start. Grid power transformed our operations, but we needed a generator. The grid power proved unreliable. Power outages were frequent. Sometimes the cause was storm damage from limbs across power lines. Perhaps a truck accident took out a pole or a transformer failed from a maintenance oversight. But the biggest problem was that Uganda had more power demand than capacity. Blink. No power. To meet the electrical needs in one area of the country power would be turned off in another, maybe for just a few hours, but sometimes for days.

When you have power, you depend on it. An example: We built a computer lab with thirty computers so a class of thirty students all had a working computer. For Northern Uganda this was unprecedented. No other school had that many working computers. But this impressive computer lab was rendered useless when the power went off.

So we had a growing desire for a generator that could be switched on, to give us uninterrupted power.

Unbeknownst to me, a donor, wishing to remain anonymous, had contacted our US staff, pledging to purchase a generator for Otino Waa. I received a call from Jim, our Accounts Manager, asking me to research how big a generator we needed. Some time had passed and Jim called again, this time with more urgency. Like, "Get on this! Get a price for the generator big enough to do the job now and in the future." I got the message! I found a new 30 KW diesel unit in Kampala, I reported back to Jim, and the price was $18,000! He quickly responded, "Buy it, money is in the bank!" The news was overwhelming. Wonderful and overwhelming!

We poured a concrete slab and after the generator was installed, an enclosure was built to keep it secure. Joseph connected a cross-over switch, allowing us to easily switch on the generator when grid power failed. Power was back on with little delay. It just purred along under no strain. Its capacity to deliver far exceeded the demands we placed on it.

Getting electrical power was a three-part journey. Solar power got us started, grid power changed our ability to operate, and the backup generator filled the power gaps. A reliable power system kept motors running and lights on. What a marvelous example of the needs of orphans and widows being met by the generosity of God-directed disciples. The needy and the generous, engaged in His divine plan. It was wonderful to behold!

The back-up generator kept us powered up during the frequent outages.

>> Chapter 19

TOWN OFFICE

Soon after Otino Waa opened, Carol and I moved to Lira from Kampala and rented some space for a desk or two for our office. School Block One put us in the education sector, a whole new area of involvement.

It became increasingly evident that we needed a town office from which to do the expanding work at hand. Reverend Dickens started searching for land of suitable size and location. He also knew the city could grant property to organizations that were established and were a true benefit to the community. When he submitted our proposal to the officials it gained their approval and we were given a 49-year lease for a parcel of land in a secure area of Lira. This was fantastic news! We had been given a great property for an office. Well, it was officially free, but we were required to pay a "premium", which covered other unspecified things. That cost was low in comparison to the value of the land. We gladly paid for it.

We had a plot map from the city surveyor's office which gave dimensions and corner locations of the property. We located three corner pegs but could not find a marker for the fourth corner. We needed the city surveyor to set the fourth corner marker, so we could be assured of the boundaries before the building started. It would be an easy task, maybe take half an hour. But he was elusive! He was either out in the field, not back from holiday break, very busy on another project, or we just missed him going to lunch (It was four o'clock). Checking in at his office for weeks, a month, then six weeks, brought us no results. Several words came to mind – frustrated, irritated, agitated--and patience was long gone. Feeling I had exhausted all avenues of getting the surveyor's cooperation, I turned to Jude, a local attorney who had befriended us. It was amazing how motivating a letter from the law office was. Only days later the surveyor was there, but he was fired up mad. We had a lawyer on his case and he was angry. Now he was the one who was irritated. He set the corner peg and left in a huff.

We set our minds to planning. The town office would be a multi-purpose building. It would have a reception area with a secretary desk, a main office, a cafe with several seating options, a gift shop, toilets, and two self-contained rooms to rent. Plans were drawn, revised, finalized, and submitted to the city building department.

But, the plans were rejected. Drawn with a T-square and triangle was not good enough. (They were perfectly fine). The plans had to be computer drawn. To my amazement, I found an office in Lira with the equipment and trained draftsmen to draw the plans. When it came to the pitch of the roof, he had a real problem. He insisted on a steeper roof. When asked why the steeper roof, he re plied, "It was to handle the rain load." What? Rain would accumulate on the roof? Water would linger? Think about it. Pour a glass of water on any slanted surface and see if it hesitates to run off. Does it get an inch deep before it will run off? He very reluctantly drew it to my specifications.

The revised plans were resubmitted, but now there was a new problem. An architect's stamp was required, showing his approval. There were no architects in Lira and very few in Kampala. It would be almost impossible to comply and everyone knew it. But we managed to submit our plans to a Kampala architect. We showed our intent to comply.

With plans in hand and a long measuring tape, Carol and I located the building on the property. There was room for parking in front, access on both sides and room enough behind for a future director's home. It was a great day when the masons arrived and the foundations were dug. The weeks following were a beehive of activity as the building took form.

Every few weeks, the city building inspector would drop by the site and look things over. We assured him the plans were in the hands of the architect and we were still waiting for his stamp of approval. As we waited, the building was going ahead without delay. We were still waiting to hear from the architect as the finishing touches brought the town office to completion. We tried to comply, the inspector was happy, he got his fee, we were happy, and the town office was move-in ready. We never did hear from the architect.

A set of plans directs the builders, but not everything is foreseen in every detail. The plans showed an arched opening between the kitchen and the customer ordering area. The masons noted the opening was arched and followed the plan. The missing detail was the height of the arch above the counter. An abrupt halt was called when I saw the arched opening was about chest high. A person would have to be on their knees to see in and order what they wanted.

It was rebuilt, with the arch well above eye level to everyone's satisfaction. Yes, it had been built according to the plan. It was just a surprise to me that no one questioned the construction, even though it was totally impractical. No one stood back, looked at it, and thought, will this really work? We better ask, to be sure.

The Town Office in Lira, Uganda

The completed town office gave us space to conduct all our business. The office secretary greeted all who entered. The director had a private office to transact all business. The well-stocked gift shop enticed travelers and locals to take a look. The cafe served up cinnamon rolls, ice cream, as well as complete meals. The rooms to rent provided comfortable and secure lodging. The town office, with all that going on, showed onlookers we were there to stay. We were established and serious and could be counted on. It gave us a tangible presence and a look of permanence. From then on, city and district officials accepted PATH Ministries as serious members of the community.

Having an office to work from was a big step forward. It helped us in so many ways. We were more settled and able to carry out the many business details that came our way each day. It was a necessary and wonderful building.

>> Chapter 20

ILERA COMMUNITY CHURCH

We had been totally focused on finishing Circle One in time to receive the initial seventy-eight orphans. We barely made it. After they arrived we had barely caught our breath, when we realized Sunday was upon us and we were unprepared. We had been so consumed with the needs of the day, that Sunday was a future event to be dealt with later. Later was now upon us, as we scrambled to hold church at Otino Waa for the first time.

A blue tarp was attached to the Otingaling Shop, our shop for kids' supplies, stretching to nearby trees. Tied in place, it gave enough shade for the morning service. Two or three African drums gave us a beat and young voices filled our small space with familiar songs. So, from the first week, the pattern was set. There would be church every week from then on. Preaching from Rev. Dickens brought spiritual focus and instruction, so their young souls were nourished with the truths of scripture.

Each Sunday, the drums and singing could be heard by close neighbors and soon, some were joining us. Our start-up church was slowly growing. Composed of the orphaned children, the house moms, and several staff members, we numbered 90 + people. The community group was 20, then 30, quickly reaching 50.

After church, it was lunchtime for Otino Waa and the community stayed on and ate too. When the number of community people was small, everyone sharing the meal was fine. But feeding an extra 50 was a bit much! It was time to make some changes.

Pastor Douglas and Rev. Dickens made inquiries of neighborhood property owners, to see if anyone had land to sell for a church building. A one-acre parcel directly across the highway from the entrance to Otino Waa was a perfect location and, after much negotiating, it was purchased. We were in Ilera Parish, so the church was named Ilera Community Church. The land purchase was privately funded, so no money came from donations to Otino Waa. The church was financially and organizationally separate from Otino Waa. It is its own entity.

Soon funds became available for building the first phase of the church. It was a simple shed roof. That gave the needed shade and basic structure, to hold church in our brand new spot. There was a physical separation between Otino Waa and Ilera Church, which solved the problem of the community staying for lunch. Everyone went home after church.

The shed roof was soon too small, so phase two of church construction added a second shed, connecting at the ridge, making a complete gable roof. A stage, three steps above the main floor, increased the visibility of the speakers and worship team. And a generator-powered sound system insured all could hear the singers and those speaking.

Pavers were eventually added to the dirt floor to keep the dust down. Feet stomping (on the devil) and dancing and moving to the energetic music, raised quite a cloud. Pavers were a wonderful addition.

Young and old filled Ilera Church as Bible truths were taught in English and Luo.

People came walking from all directions, drawn by the music and the warm welcome. Neighbors invited neighbors and once they came they stayed. They heard many topics, preached from the Bible, which was refreshing and encouraging. Each week, a person could receive prayer for salvation, forgiveness, healing, or deliverance. They came burdened and troubled and left refreshed and set free.

The church gained the reputation of being a place that welcomed all, whatever their church background. There was no scolding or pressuring about attendance or giving or loyalty of any sort. They were loved and accepted and helped. They found the love of other people and the love of God.

The church continued to grow in number, as Circle Two and Circle Three were added at Otino Waa. Community attendance increased as well. Rev. Dickens led the church with Pastor Douglas as his very able second-in-command. They were very intentional, as they wove the Otino Waa attendees together with the community members. Leaders were trained and given jobs to do. There were no distinctions made, all served where asked. Mothers from Otino Waa led groups, and community members also led. Church members mixed freely.

Carol and I had received training in the US in setting up small groups within the church to deepen relationships. The early church, of the Bible, met from house to house and also in the temple. That was the model for small groups meeting in homes and meeting on Sunday at Ilera Church. We didn't know of any church in the area that used that model of ministry, but we saw real advantages to it. Discussions with Rev. Dickens and Pastor Douglas brought us to a consensus to try it at our church.

The church was growing, quickly reaching three to four hundred. Rev. Dickens and Pastor Douglas were the only church staff. It was impossible for them to meet the needs of that many people. Trained small group leaders could lighten their load. So, a meeting was called, for those who might be interested in more church involvement. Small group leaders were the key to establishing groups. We were on the hunt for those potential leaders. The concept of small groups, meeting in homes (huts), led by church people, building relationships during the week, and discussing the previous week's sermon was laid out. Then, they were asked, "Would you like to be trained to be such a leader?"

This idea was overwhelming. How could they lead a group? They were not trained in Bible knowledge. How could they answer questions about church or God? How could they lead a group, when they had never even learned to read? Lots of questions.

We assured them they didn't have to know everything. We would train them in how to present salvation, how to present baptism, how to lead the weekly meeting, and how to report back each Sunday. When topics or questions came up that they could not answer, they should say they didn't know but would find out. Those answers would come from Rev. Dickens or Pastor Douglas. We assured them it would work, they could learn, and God would use them.

There was timid hesitation, but some stepped up to become small group leaders, groups formed, and we had a start. With ongoing training, confidence was rising, and the leaders developed. They didn't need a degree in theology to pray, and they prayed. There was healing, salvation, deliverance from evil spirits, and release from fears.

The small group leaders became the first line of ministry for the church. If someone came to me with a problem, my first question was, "Have you talked with your small group leader?" Start there, and if they still needed help they would ask Douglas. These leaders reduced the workload on Rev. Dickens and Douglas immensely.

Ephesians 5:12 has, "Equipping the saints for the work of service". That verse was in full swing at Ilera Church.

As this model of ministry took shape, I learned that even an illiterate person could lead a group. One of the ladies in our leadership team could neither read nor write. She invited one of the Otino Waa house moms to attend her group. The mom would read the scripture and the group leader took it from there. She couldn't read but she was a keen listener of the previous sermon. She could direct a discussion and pray with authority.

Every week, special music was provided by a group of Otino Waa kids. Even the six and seven-year-olds. With direction from their moms, they would file onto the stage. The keyboard player started playing and their prepared song rang forth. One or two of them had a mic and they sang it out with amazing confidence. It was always a positive part of the morning worship, people loved it.

When new children came to Otino Waa, many were suffering from some sort of trauma. It could have been parents dying, being abandoned, unwanted, or ill-treated by relatives, or being neglected in a child-headed household. They were scared, insecure, traumatized little kids.

On Sunday mornings everyone, except the guards, went to church. Any child staying behind would have been unsupervised. That was not an option. So, the new child would be in church, but very withdrawn. Body language said a lot. They stood, looking down with arms crossed, tightly holding themselves. But being in church was trauma therapy on several levels. First, was the atmosphere of exalting God with African-style robust singing. Everyone was in mo tion. With arms raised, feet in motion, and bodies swaying, from the very young to the oldest in attendance. All across the church, it was like that. They were surrounded by music and motion.

Added to that, was the spirit of God ministering to their hurts. They were receiving love from their mom and housemates, Bible words were touching their hearts, and prayer was working.

I don't know why, but six weeks in church seems to have had a dramatic effect on their whole demeanor. It was a visible change. Their arms relaxed and hung loosely at their sides. Their bodies moved slightly to the beat of the music, then raised hands followed. Week by week, they experienced more freedom. And around six weeks they would come for prayer at the end of the service. Somehow, all those components brought healing and restoration to those traumatized young lives. I saw it happen over and over again.

Church became packed so expansion was planned. Floor space would be doubled, plus two small offices and secure storage for the sound system and instruments were planned. Funds came in from visiting teams, friends, and churches. When finished, it seemed huge, but the new benches quickly filled up, so we made more. This was outstanding! A typical village church was 30 to 50. The Ilera Church had six hundred and some Sundays seven hundred. We counted!

We started with seventy-eight orphans, their moms, a couple drums, and an overhead tarp. Now, the church had a sizable building. Trained leaders were actively engaged in small groups, in village outreach, in swamp baptism, and in preaching. They learned to pray with authority. It was very thrilling to be part of such a thriving church!

The Ilera church had a powerful effect on the Otino Waa kids. They all attended every Sunday until they graduated and left. The preaching was strictly Bible-based. Rev. Dickens preached, as did Pastor Douglas and Carol and I (about once a month). This variety brought different styles of presentation, changes in tempo, and emphasis. It kept interest high. They learned verses, precepts, and correct theology, and through it, became fervent solid Christians. They often led the spiritual thrust wherever they went. They were known for their God-centered lives and testimony. I thank God for the spiritual leadership Rev. Dickens brought to the church. Because of him, the church thrived.

Ilera Church served the children and staff of Otino Waa as well as the surrounding community.

Offerings at Ilera Church were unique to my experience. At the end of the morning service, all were invited to bring their offering. Some had a coin or two, and a few had something more substantial.

The Otino Waa kids and moms had Owallings (more on that later), and others brought an ear of corn or an egg, or a chicken. Then the weekly auction turned the in-kind offerings into cash. Owallings were redeemed for Uganda Shillings, and farm-fresh offerings were auctioned for cash. Everyone participated in their own way – tailored to the community culture.

What a thrill, every Sunday morning, to see people come walking to church from every direction. Our humble beginning of a drum and tarp had turned into a dynamic church ministering to all comers!

>> Chapter 21

THE BEASON FAMILY

Joey and Ruthie Beason brought a short-term mission team from Cottonwood Church, in Southern California, in 2003, to Otino Waa to give us a much-needed helping hand. Circle One was under construction and we were racing to get all ten houses and the kitchen built in time to receive the first children. The orphans were coming at the end of the school term, which was rapidly approaching. Without the team's help, we would have not been ready.

As Joey and Ruthie returned home to California, they continued to think about Otino Waa and all that we were facing. They felt drawn to the project and after prayerful consideration, gave us a call. "We want to move to Uganda for two years and help you at Otino Waa. Would that be okay?" The call left us speechless! We couldn't believe they would be willing to uproot their life and move with four small boys, to help us. Our response was an emphatic, "Yes, please come!"

They arrived in Lira and settled into a rental house. It didn't take long for them to fully engage in Otino Waa life. School Block One was under construction and Joey became the project manager. He coordinated with Salva, our Ugandan contractor, to see that all the details of construction were in order. That was our largest building to date, so there was a lot to learn. Joey's help was of immense value.

Each Sunday, many community children, as well as the Otino Waa kids, were at church. Joey and Ruthie took charge of all the younger kids, five to eight-year-olds. They held children's church in the large room of the Otino Waa Office. They sang, prayed, and did puppet lessons, with the older Otino Waa kids as helpers. It was an exciting, fun, and God-saturated time together. Everyone loved it! They made God come alive in those young eager hearts.

The Beason boys soon made friends with their Otino Waa age mates. They would be off in every direction with their newfound friends. Ruthie didn't have to worry about where they were as the house moms were watching the antics of all the busy boys. They were safe within the confines of Otino Waa, even if they were out of sight.

Ruthie's days were filled with homeschooling. To keep four boys of different ages progressing through all subjects demanded her full attention. Add to that, three meals a day for hungry growing boys. She was a busy mom!

Whatever needed doing, they were there to help. They hosted the visiting short-term church teams, put on movie nights, hauled people around, delivered supplies, and helped with building the Ilera Church.

Their friendship was so important to us, as well. It was so encouraging to have someone to share a friendly visit with, or talk out a problem with, to have a laugh with. It was so good having them with us. We really needed them! We truly felt God had sent them our way at just the right time. We don't know how we would have done it without them.

Joey & Ruthie Beason were invaluable to the work in those days.

>> Chapter 22

PRINTING OUR OWN MONEY

When the first 78 Otino Waa kids arrived it came to our immediate attention that we needed a system for them to get basic supplies like soap, toothpaste, or a plastic plate if they lost theirs. If we freely handed out supplies with every request there would be no control. We needed some way of supplying their needs, and at the same time teaching personal responsibility.

Carol and I were in our Land Cruiser talking this over as we traveled. A God-inspired idea popped into our minds. It went something like this: What if we created our own currency which could only be spent at Otino Waa? It could be equivalent in value to the Uganda Shilling, so it would seem almost like real money. Supplies could be stocked and put on sale to be purchased. Each child would be given a set amount each month so they could buy what they needed.

This would teach financial responsibility, would be self-regulating (out of money, out of luck), and would be an orderly way for everyone to get supplies.

The first step to make this happen was to buy a 20-foot container. This was perfect. It was big enough to hold all the necessary supplies. It was watertight, termite-proof, and had secure locking doors.

The container was delivered and was leveled using truck wheels at each corner to get it up out of the dirt. Shelves were installed, then supplies made the little shop ready for business. The "Otingaling Shop" was born!

The new currency was an Owalling and could only be spent at the Otingaling Shop. Carol designed the bills of various amounts and we had them printed in Kampala at Vincent's print shop. He printed and cut them to size. Since he could print money, I guess that made him the Treasury Department for Otino Waa.

These children were orphans from the village and had never had any money. So there was a big learning curve. Getting them from a penniless orphan to a child with cash needing to buy their basic supplies of bathing soap, laundry soap, and toothpaste took a lot of instruction.

A staff member was put in charge of purchasing all the needed supplies, (a few candies were even on the shelf) and posting when the store would be open. This was a whole new experience! They had to learn to make their money last all month, buy essentials first, and save a little if they wanted something special that cost more.

There were many very young kids, so their house mom had to help them and take care of their Owallings. As the weeks turned into months, they learned the value of their money, the prices of each item, and that there were choices they could make.

For instance; when Matthew, the Otingaling Manager, shopped for bathing soap for the store, he bought several brands. They could choose the brand they wanted. This allowed for personal preference and individual expression.

We printed our own money (Owallings) which could only be spent at the Otingaling Shop in Otino Waa.

It was a thrill to see the system working! Since it was working well for the kids, we expanded the system to include the moms and other staff. It was a small perk that helped them out with basic supplies.

In the course of Sunday morning teaching, there was instruction about giving. Owallings provided us with the perfect tool to teach about tithing. The concept of the 10% tithe was one topic among many. Since all the children received Owallings each month, they all had real money, (real in their world), so they could actually give to God. They thought about it, considered it, and eventually some started giving.

Then Owallings started to show up in the offering. Think of that! What thrilling stuff for orphans to be giving of their own very limited money. This was evidence of personal commitment. They were able to be a vital part of their church by obedience in giving.

Owallings were carefully collected and counted. The church could not spend that currency, but the giving was genuine and real. So, at the end of the month, Carol and I exchanged Shillings for their Owallings. That turned their offering into spendable cash. Owallings were put back into circulation and we were delighted to see the system working at Otino Waa and Ilera Church.

I could hardly believe we ran into this next problem. We were just an orphanage out in a village setting in Northern Uganda. Hardly a high-profile place!

As mentioned earlier, some staff also received Owallings, which could be used to purchase items from the Otingaling Store. It came to our attention that one of the guards was spending a lot at our store. How did he have such purchasing power? Where did he get all the in-house money?

When called into Rev. Dickens' office, it soon came out that he had taken samples of Owallings to the town copy machine. We had a counterfeiter in our ranks! I had to laugh at the thought of our homespun money entering the clandestine world of counterfeiting.

He readily repented in great humility. He promised to never again do such a thing. Rev. Dickens knew he was not an evil man at heart, just poor. He was given a second chance, was not fired, and continued to work faithfully for many more years.

The next time Vincent printed Owallings for us, he used a special paper, called Vellum. It is a heavy paper, nearly transparent. It was not available in Lira, so this was an upgrade to our currency, ensuring our money was tamper-proof, sort of.

Creating our own monetary system was an idea we had no inkling of beforehand. But we had a problem to solve. We were in deep consideration of finding a solution and God gave us direction. From there it took shape, was refined over time, and served us well. You never know what problems may arise. My conclusion, from this experience, would be to give an issue your full attention, but still leave room for a degree of intervention from Almighty God!

Chapter 23

IMPROVED SPRINGS

Clean drinking water is essential for survival. A foundational basic human need. What could be a greater necessity than water? We take safe water for granted living in the US. But living in Uganda, outside the city, clean water is a huge need.

Some regions of Northern Uganda have naturally occurring springs. Clean water flows out of the ground, but there is an immediate problem. The land is only slightly hilly. So as the water flows there is little fall to the ground level. A pool of water develops since there is scant drainage. The clean water from the spring produces a stagnant, scum-filled frog pond.

Cattle and people wade into the pond to access the water. An arm swept across the surface clears most of the scum and debris so mostly clean water can be collected in a jerry can or basin. Being the best water available draws beasts and villagers alike.

In this scenario, there is inevitable contamination. Waterborne typhoid, dysentery, and cholera are serious threats. Poor sanitation spreads intestinal worms throughout the village. This wonderful source of pure water needs to be captured before it is contaminated.

A scummy pond was the best water available before it was "improved."

There are Ugandan teams trained in the procedure of transforming these springs into a source of pure water flowing from a pipe. The first step is to evaluate a spring location to see if there is enough slope to drain the water away from the spring. If so, a channel is dug to drain the pond which will expose the eye of the spring flowing out of the bank. That area is cleared so the water flows freely. Slightly below the spring opening several layers are laid down. First a layer of clay is applied to seal the water from seeping down. Then crushed rock and sand are added which acts as a filter. A brick retaining wall is built with a two-inch pipe extending through it. Gravity feed directs the spring water over the clay, through the crushed rock and sand. Uncontaminated pure water now flows through the pipe being the only outlet through the retaining wall.

The pipe is high enough to allow a jerry can to be placed there for filling. A channel is dug draining excess water away from the area. The immediate area, from the retaining wall downstream several feet, is bricked and cemented to prevent erosion.

Provision is made in the downstream area for pot or clothes washing and cattle watering. Any possible contamination is downstream from the source of the pure spring water.

The final step is to cap the spring with clean fill material, level with the retaining wall, and fence it off to keep animals from trampling the area. That would cause recontamination of the spring.

When we saw the critical need for clean water we were attracted to this process of improving springs. It was a very doable project, for those who were properly trained. A spring could be completed in a few weeks. It was within our price range, less than $1,000 per spring. So Carol wrote an email explaining the need and the cost. What an easy project to promote; an affordable water source for 2,000 or more villagers per improved spring.

When donations came in, we identified a new spring location and turned the team loose to build it. One or two springs were being completed each month.

Contact was made with the nearby village leaders requiring them to form a water committee. They had to collect 30,000 Shillings and entrust it to the committee for spring maintenance before we would begin the project. That amount was about $12. This was their spring. We were just the installers. The goal was for them to take ownership and have pride in their community spring.

Along with the spring, we provided training in hygiene and sanitation. Deworming and clean water improved the quality of life for the whole area. Dewormed babies slept at night. Everyone was happier.

Clean water flowing out of a pipe was a wonderful improvement in village after village all across the area. It was all done in the name of Jesus. A cup of clean water in the name of Jesus blessed people, no matter what their religious beliefs.

The water team transformed the scum pond to clean pure water flowing from a pipe.

One day one of our staff members met an old man coming from a newly completed spring. When he learned that the staff member was responsible for getting the water flowing out of the pipe he addressed him with great emotion. The old man rubbed his hands all over his head and then reached over and rubbed his hands all over the staff's head. "All the blessings I have I give to you. That is the first pure water of my life." He was so choked up, as he left the old man, words just did not come. He had just witnessed true gratitude for the blessing of clean water to drink.

One hundred springs; then one hundred fifty; and then two hundred springs were completed, followed by a celebration. One by one, as the money came in, springs were completed. Over time great progress was made. Over 400,000 villagers were drinking clean spring water, flowing from a pipe, as a result of this project. This was an example of steady plodding, over time, producing a great result. Just as the scripture reminds us to be steadfast, unmovable, always abounding in the work of the Lord, for our labor is not in vain in the Lord. (1 Corinthians 15:58) Steady plodding with spring after spring produced wonderful results.

>> Chapter 24

HYDRAFORM

Carol saw an advertisement in the back of a Christian magazine for a brick-making machine. It was intriguing. It produced a 9" X 9" X 3" block made from a mixture of sand, soil, and cement. The moistened mixture was hydraulically pressed in a mold to produce a block that interlocked top and bottom and end to end. The block was stable when stacked, requiring no mortar.

The girls' POP house (People of Purpose) was designed and ready to be built. Its purpose was to give vocational training to the older girls. So a project was waiting. We were home in the US for two months and introduced the Hydraform machine during a presentation of our work in Uganda to Oasis Church, in Bend, Oregon. It was a cool idea, but it cost a bundle – $26,000. I thought, "There is no way we could ever raise that much money." It was just out of reach, out of the question.

But the folks at Oasis expressed an immediate interest. With only a bit of conversation, they committed to supply half of the cost. Already, this was way beyond any faith I had to raise that much.

Then we showed pictures and explained the machine to our friend and supporter, Milt Buehner. He could see the potential for its use as Otino Waa expanded in the years to come. He was sold on the idea, and offered to pay the other half. I was shocked! We'd only been home a few weeks and the machine was totally paid for!

On our return to Uganda, we stopped at the Hydraform office in Kampala. We were ready to buy. The basic hand-fed and hand-operated machine would suit our needs. When it was delivered they sent a trainer for a week to instruct us in its operation.

The Hydraform machine produced a building block from soil, sand, and cement. The 10 member block team could produce 500 blocks a day.

The trainer was great! He taught our ten-member Hydraform crew the correct mix of soil, sand, and cement. The moisture content had to be just right. When squeezed in the hand, it should make a ball but not leak out between the fingers.

The soil had to be screened to get the rocks out. Rocks would wear the mold sides too quickly. The screened soil was put in a heap with sand and cement. Using a hoe, the pile on the ground was mixed thoroughly.

The crew had come from villages nearby. They had no mechanical experience and never operated a machine or anything with a motor. The trainer needed to impart every detail, his trainees knew nothing.

The blocks interlocked when stacked requiring no mortar.

He made sure they got the right mixture, tested for the right moisture, and then by bucket, dumped the right amount into the mold. It was scraped flush at the mold opening. The compressing ram exerted pressure until the hydraulic gauge reached the black line. The top ram was moved to the up position. The bottom ram pushed out the newly-formed block. This precise sequence produced uniform blocks. It took all ten men working, to keep the machine productive.

Men were screening, mixing, filling the mold, operating the machine, and one man was picking and stacking the blocks in neat rows. At the end of the day, the blocks were covered with black plastic to prevent rapid drying. The stacks of blocks were watered daily for a week, to keep them hydrated. Slow curing made for stronger blocks.

It was a process, they mastered it, they were employed, and we were delighted! They produced 500 blocks a day! The formerly inexperienced crew now had a trade. They could do what no one else in all of Northern Uganda could do. They remained employed for years and years as Otino Waa added houses, schools, and a clinic.

Next, the trainer had to retrain the masons. They were very good at building with bricks and mortar, but some new skills were needed to stack interlocking blocks without mortar. He started his instruction from the ground up. The first course was set in mortar on the slab. Half blocks staggered the courses. Partitions meeting outer walls were a construction detail needing explanation. Block meeting door frames and window frames were explained. Each of the top three courses was set in mortar with strips of metal strapping in the mortar to give stability.

We were eager to start on the POP Center. While the masons poured the footings, set the stem walls, and poured the slab, the new Hydraform crew started making blocks. It didn't take long to establish a working sequence and block after block was produced. Our brand-new machine and crew were in motion and it was working! Very thrilling!

By the time the slab was ready, a neat stack of blocks was ready to be laid. Lines were snapped on the slab and the first course was carefully set level and flat in a bed of mortar. Then, starting from an outside corner, the stacking quickly grew the walls in both directions.

There was a high learning curve with this first building since it was a new technique. But block makers and masons succeeded and the new building was a beauty! The trainer had set us up for success. The finished building was testimony to his teaching ability.

Carol saw the ad; had the vision; and two donors paid for it all. The Hydraform machine arrived, training was provided, and block makers and masons proved it worked. Our new machine would produce several hundred thousand blocks in the years to come. It was a wonderful machine that made the blocks for every building built from then on.

>> **Chapter 25**

MILT

The story of Otino Waa would not be complete without mentioning Milt and Donna Buehner. It could be said, our introduction to Milt was by divine appointment. Carol was a member of a local athletic club in Bend. She was exercising on one apparatus when she noticed this man working out on another. She felt such a strong urge to meet him, she boldly approached and said, " I think I need to know you." He was taken aback by this strange woman but was gracious and engaged her in casual conversation. That was the beginning of a friendship that would last for many years

Milt was a successful businessman; a devoted Christian, committed to supporting Christian endeavors he was drawn to. As we prepared to move to Uganda, to train church leaders, Milt stepped up with a significant financial gift to help us get started.

By the end of four years, we had become established in Uganda and were successful in training church leaders in Uganda, Rwanda, and the Democratic Republic of Congo. On one of our trips back to the US, we wanted to thank Milt for believing in us and show him a PowerPoint presentation Carol had created. She called his number, but no answer. She called again. Still, no answer. Carol's persistent calls got no response. We began to wonder if he just didn't want to talk to us. Maybe he was thinking we were after more money. That was never our intent. Finally, on the thirteenth call, Milt agreed to meet over lunch. He may have felt it was the only way to stop the phone from ringing! Carol had indeed worn him down. Carol's relentless pursuit paid off. We were able to give him and Donna a proper thank you.

Milt had heard our stories about Otino Waa but he had to come and see it for himself.

Early on, in our relationship, Milt may have been apprehensive in providing his support, but in time, he came to believe God indeed had his hand on us. Especially, when it came to caring for the orphans. He often referred to the verse in James Chapter 1, about caring for orphans and widows in their distress. That is what he wanted to do! For Otino Waa, Milt became our "Patron Saint." He wanted to be sure we had what we needed to care for and educate the orphans.

From the Hydraform block machine, the science building and diesel generator at Otino Waa, the office compound, and the director's house in Lira, to the making of the documentary "Lost and Found " Milt was involved in all of it. It was unprecedented! We were blessed, humbled, and at times totally overwhelmed. It was a God-directed, economy-of-God relationship. Kingdom work is accomplished when those with the ability to give, connect with those in the field needing support. What a marvelous connection that was!

>> Chapter 26

CIRCLE TWO

Circle One's homes were established and running smoothly. But we realized that we also had many needy orphans on our waiting list, so we decided that we must begin building the homes of Circle Two. Once again we needed to make plans in faith.

Carol called our friend and former pastor in Oregon and explained the need to her because she had been a support to us and a prayer partner. "This is a big project," our friend said, "I don't have much faith that I know anyone to talk to about such a need. But I will pray, " she told Carol, "and let's see if the Lord shows up."

Just two days later, that Pastor friend received a call from an acquaintance who worked at an agency in California named Assist International. Assist at that time was working only with the great needs in Eastern Europe, but they had been contacted by a woman who had a heart to build something in Africa. The Assist team had heard our friend speak about a very reputable ministry in Uganda called Otino Waa.

The woman named Lisa wanted to give to a trustworthy project, and she asked to make a quick trip to Uganda to see the orphanage with her own eyes. Our friend explained to her that it would be difficult to make a "quick trip " to the north of Uganda, but the details were worked out for Lisa to visit us and take time off from the start-up company she worked for in California.

When she arrived, she met the students and toured the grounds, and Carol explained to her that each of the needed houses in Circle Two would cost approximately $8900. To our surprise, she committed to funding all eight houses! The news was stunning! Dreaming was suddenly becoming a reality.

Carol called our friend in Oregon that very day with the news and said, "Guess what! You didn't know it but you 'Googled' us!" From a truly unexpected source, the Lord had worked on our behalf once again.

This put all sorts of planning into play. Circle Two needed to be separated from Circle One, but not too far. The water system needed to be extended. The brush needed to be cleared. And we were rethinking the house design. I drew a new house plan with three major changes. The first change was to include a kitchen.

In Circle One, a central kitchen provided food for all ten houses. That kitchen arrangement worked, but our thinking was changing. If each house had its own kitchen, there would be several benefits. It would create a family atmosphere of eight children and a mom cooking together. Cooking skills would be learned by everyone, clean-up would be shared, and more cohesive relations would develop as they worked together as a family.

The second change would be a bathing room in the house. It too, would build a sense of belonging to the house and to the house members. A more personalized feel to it.

The third major change was to have a toilet in the house, to be used only by the eight kids and their Mom. This was a definite upgrade in sanitation.

The standard toilet in rural settings is a pit latrine; a deep hole in the ground covered with a floor with an eight-inch hole in the center. Very basic, but they serve their purpose and are better than no toilet at all. The drawbacks are evident from afar. They are very smelly and unpleasant for all who enter. And there are flies, by the swarm. Keeping them clean is nearly impossible. This had to do with poor aim and alignment with the aforementioned hole. This toilet talk is not very pleasant for a great conversation. But it is essential infrastructure. Let's face it, people need to poop!

So the toilet in the house would not be a pit. Research revealed other possibilities. A few model toilets had been built, which we examined. Nothing fit our situation exactly, but the idea was there. The design we chose was an Eco-San toilet. A composting toilet, which we adapted to fit our nine-person house. I had just become a poop engineer!

The concept started with the toilet floor. It was designed with a hole for the feces and raised footprints for foot placement. This guaranteed correct alignment. In front of that, the floor was funnel-shaped, leading to a small hole. The hole directed urine to a specific destination.

When feces and urine are separated, there is much less offensive odor. A very big benefit! The urine is disposed of in a simple drain field, while the feces is collected in a container. On schedule, the container is emptied onto a cement slab, dried over time, and then composted with wood shavings. It is then used for crop fertilizer, but not root crops like carrots or potatoes.

The concept had to be refined to fit our application of a nine-person household. In Kampala, the company that made our large plastic water tanks also made an Eco-San molded plastic toilet floor. It was made of sturdy plastic, about 4 feet by 4 feet, molded in the correct design, with a lid to seal the large hole. The lid had a molded toe loop for easy hands-free, removal and replacement. It was smooth plastic, easy for cleaning. All smooth easy-to-clean plastic.

The plastic company also made a plastic tub, a little smaller than the floor size. At two feet deep, it had the capacity for a week's output from the house. Wondering? How is that known? It was data collected by the poop engineer!

As the house was built, the molded floor was installed high enough to allow the tub to slide under it for collection. The door to the outside could be opened to remove the tub and replace it with an empty, one each week.

The urine collector was piped to the outside and emptied into a trench filled with large drain rock, topped with dirt to ground level.

Cooking in the house is done with charcoal, which produces ash. The ash, when cool, is collected in a large can and placed in the corner of the toilet. When toilet time is completed, before replacing the toe loop lid, a scoop of ash is added. The ash has a drying effect and changes the pH, which kills off harmful microbes.

Circle Two houses had their own kitchen, mother's room, bedroom area for 8, bathing room, & Eco-San toilet. The new design created a cohesive family unit.

It took some serious searching to learn the details of this new toilet system. We had not found a working model to pattern after, so this was new territory for us. When Circle Two was completed, our newly designed houses were put to the test. Food was being cooked in the kitchens, the bathing area was being used, and the new toilet needed some initial instructions for use. No one had seen anything like it, nor had we.

Use for a month was enough time for an evaluation. The toilet door was flung open and not one fly was buzzing. That alone was fantastic! And even sniffing didn't detect foul odors. That was nearly unbelievable! The easy-to-clean floor was indeed clean. The system worked, much to our delight. We were the first in rural Northern Uganda to have such marvelous toilets. The Eco-San was a vast improvement over the pit latrine. We were committed to the new toilet design. Any new house built in the future was Eco-San equipped.

Essential to each new house being built were the house moms. To qualify as an Otino Waa house mom, the applicant needed to be single. Most were widows. It was required that they be Christian, so they could provide their kids with spiritual guidance. The ability to speak English and have at least a primary school education was another requirement. If they had children of their own, depending on their age, they could bring one to live in the house with them. Having dedicated mothers was vital for the children's adjustment, growth, and well-being. She cared for them, loved them, trained

them and cooked for them. She became the mom they may never have had. The loving care the children received from their moms nourished their traumatized souls and gave them stability. They could relax and just be kids again. Indeed, the moms of Otino Waa deserve to be honored for their contribution to raising the hundreds of Otino Waa graduates.

>> Chapter 27
SHORT-TERM TEAMS

Carol and I came home once a year to rest and recuperate. But, as Otino Waa became established, our time back in the US was spent traveling and speaking at churches around the Northwest. As interest in Otino Waa grew, some of these churches began sending teams. Hosting those teams became a huge part of our ministry.

The team leader has his work cut out as he prepares his team. It takes planning and a lot of fundraising to get a team ready for a mission trip. Preparations include getting plane tickets, passports, vaccinations, meds, gifts for orphans, and supplies for projects. Everything needed there needs to be bought in the US, packed in suitcases, and carried to Uganda. The total cost per individual could be $3,000 plus or minus.

 A good team leader would also alert his team to the cultural nuances they will encounter. Language, currency, and behaviors are unique in a foreign country. Acceptable dress codes in the US can be offensive to some outside the US. In rural Uganda, girls and women never wear pants, always a dress or skirt. To show respect for this cultural norm, female team members are required to dress to that standard.

We tried to match the skills of team members to the projects we were working on. Construction workers helped build houses and a school building. Some helped pour the patio slabs for the open-air cafe dining area. Teachers held workshops for our teaching staff, introducing different ideas and teaching techniques. Dental teams came with supplies and equipment and addressed a host of issues among the children and staff too! News of an American doctor putting on a free health clinic draws villagers from miles around.

Teams were limited in size by our ability to provide transportation. Ten people and their luggage fit in our medium-sized bus. Teams stayed in Lira during the week and with two vehicles we would pick them up in the morning for the ten-mile trip to Otino Waa.

We understood the sacrifice, both in time and money, the teams made to come halfway around the world, so their time at Otino Waa needed to be as fruitful as possible. Keeping ten visitors busy and productive with projects ranging from dentistry and doctoring, to guitar lessons, to Bible studies, to construction projects, often at the same time, was always a challenge, and exhausting!

Breakfast is served at the town hotel where teams stay. Lunch at Otino Waa is a special time for bonding. Each team member is assigned to a specific kids' house and they have lunch all week at that same house. The kids and their moms love it! With names being repeated, the team soon knows all the kids' names in their house. Those faces that all look the same on day one, are soon individuals with personalities showing through.

At lunchtime, the kids track down their guests, take them by the hand and lead them to their houses. About two days of that and the team members' hearts have melted. During the time of eating beans and posho, looking at US photos, and the kids singing, two cultures, extend hospitality and receive hospitality. By the end of the week, love flows, hearts have bonded, and tears flow when the team has to depart.

A short-term team poses on the playground equipment they successfully built.

Evening meals at the Otino Waa Cafe start off with a dance team of twelve to fifteen older boys and girls in a traditional African dance. Adorned with colorful outfits and ankle bells, their bare feet move to the beat of the African drum. Chants and shrill whistles direct them through each stage of dance. It is enthusiastic and authentic.

Carol's trained vocational caterers serve buffet dishes of chicken, African fruit salad, potatoes, peanut honey sauce, and cabbage salad. For drinks, there is a choice of sodas. It's always a lovely evening and meal.

Teams can also experience Indian cuisine at Washing Bay Indian Restaurant or dine at the Town Office Cafe. A favorite is a dinner at the homes of Rev. Dickens or Pastor Douglas. Great food, just different from home. "Try this goat. It is tender and tasty. The ant paste is a little crunchy."

We felt it was important for teams to experience more than just life at Otino Waa. Side trips to the baby home, in Lira, to cuddle and pray for abandoned or orphaned babies that have been rescued; an inspection of one of the many community springs PATH has developed, providing clean fresh drinking water; a walk through Lira to the open air market, displaying all manner of produce; bananas, mangoes, papaya, carrots, cabbage and tomatoes. Fresh tilapia, dried fish, hanging sides of beef and goat, covered with flies, ready to be hacked with a machete to fill a customer's order. An abundance of flies confronts the eyes and nose.

On Sundays, teams have the opportunity to share in worship services at the Ilera Community Church, just across the road from Otino Waa. All of Otino Waa is there, numbering about 300.

The surrounding community loves this church and they come walking from every direction, adding another 300 plus. There's always a group of Otino Waa kids, big and small, bringing special music. The whole congregation is engaged, from the very young to the very old. Solid Biblical truth is preached in English and translated into Luo. At the end of each service, there is a prayer for any needing salvation, healing, or deliverance. The service concludes with the offering being received. A chicken, some eggs, some vegetables, or a goat are given and then auctioned for cash. To the joy and amazement of the Ugandans, team members often bid against one another for an item and then donate it to someone in need.

After church and tearful goodbyes, the team boards the bus for their final African adventure. About three hours from Otino Waa is Murchison Falls National Park, a game park and wildlife refuge. The team stays at Paraa Safari Lodge on the Nile River. It's a beautiful hotel, built in 1954 by the British, where teams can relax, and enjoy excellent food and accommodations. The guided game safari finds an elephant, giraffe, warthog, waterbuck, the dangerous water buffalo, and if fortunate, a pride of lions or leopards is spotted. On the boat ride up the Nile to view Murchison Falls, teams encounter hippos, crocodiles, and numerous waterfowl.

These two weeks in Uganda give a team member a lot to think about on the long trip home. Experiencing African culture; its poverty, its orphans, its open-air markets with strange foods; simple but dynamic church, is a lot to process.

We were blessed and helped by the short-term teams. They made a difference in our development and progress. We are so very grateful for the teams. Our hope is that they returned home changed by their visit, perhaps having a wider view of God at work at home, and in Africa.

>> Chapter 28

SNAKES

While living in Uganda we didn't encounter many snakes, but there were a few. Poisonous ones caught our attention, for sure! There were adders and cobras, black and green mambas that were fast enough to chase you!

A short-term missions team from Central Oregon came to help out for a week. We invited them for an evening at our house in Lira. As we entered the house, Carol found a note left by Judith, our house girl. The note was short but caught our full attention. Judith had written, " A snake was on your bed. I could not find it."

Instantly, we were on high alert. We were checking every step we took. Obvious questions sprung to mind. What color was it? Green, as in Green Mamba? How big was it? Where did you look?

Every corner of the house was checked, and the mattresses came off. Every bed was checked multiple times. Every movable chair, couch, and table was carefully inspected. All of that, but no snake was found. Was it hiding somewhere or had it crawled under a door and left the house?

After a thorough search, nothing more could be done, so the team left and went to their hotel. It was bedtime, but a certain tension remained with us. We shook our pillows, flapped the blankets, and finally crawled in for the night. We never did find our house snake. From that night on, Carol never put on a shoe without shaking it, in case a snake was curled up inside. She wanted no snake surprises!

One day, I was working in my office in our house in Lira. I heard a commotion outside, so I went out to see what was going on. Our gardener was very excited, for he had spotted a large snake and was trying to kill it. I joined the search. Sometimes it was visible, sometimes it was hidden in the grass and leaves. It was going along the compound wall looking for a way out. When it came to an obstacle it turned and faced us. Mr. Cobra raised his head about three feet high, looked at us, flicked his tongue, and flared wide his upper body, in true cobra style. We stepped back immediately! Facing a flared cobra in my yard made a lasting impression!

The gardener clobbered him with a brick and that ended the chase. Held up on a stick, he was about seven feet long. That was an impressive snake!

The Beason family, from Southern California, moved to Uganda for two years, to help us at Otino Waa. What a great help they were! They rented a house a block up the road from us. One day Ruthie, the mom, went to use the toilet. When she lifted the lid she was greeted by a snake looking up at her. It had crawled up the sewer pipe and was poking its head up from the toilet. Imagine her shock and horror when she faced this intruder. "My toilet isn't snake-proof?" "Can I ever use it again, without fear of being bitten on my bottom?" After that, the sewer pipe inspection covers were adjusted and sealed, making it a closed system and safe. Then a chemical, toxic to snakes, was flushed down the toilet. Even though the family was assured the problem was solved, for weeks, any toilet time was brief and accompanied by residual anxiety!

Having this much cobra in our yard caused intense excitement. That was the one and only time I faced a flared cobra looking at me flicking his tongue.

>> Chapter 29

VOCATIONAL TRAINING

Otino Waa was a safe haven for some of the most vulnerable children in the area. They were orphans with almost nothing. But they got a bed to sleep in, food to eat, clothes to wear, a "mother" to love them, and they were safe. Having that level of care was a major improvement in their lives, life-changing.

Their physical needs were being met and the church brought them spiritual nourishment. They learned there was a God and that He loved them. Through Jesus, their sins could be forgiven and they could have peace in their heart. They came to understand many truths of the Bible.

To rise above poverty, to do more than barely exist, they needed an education. Otino Waa Primary School and Secondary Schools were started to provide that. They attended class, they learned, and they gained confidence that they were as good a student as any in the district. It was a major accomplishment, to develop a place that met their physical needs, enriched their spiritual life, and provided both primary and secondary education. But, as the older ones were about to graduate, we realized they were completing their classes, but had no practical skills. They needed job skills, so we started vocational classes. The areas chosen were woodworking, cooking and catering, beekeeping, sewing, agriculture, and computer training. A rotation schedule was set up, so the older students got exposure in each of these areas. It sounds simple enough, but it was a huge endeavor.

To set up the woodworking class, tools were needed. Multiples of each tool – saws, planes, chisels, try squares, framing squares, hammers, measuring tapes, and drills. Some tools came as donations from US teams, some were bought in Kampala, and some from Lira. Securing the tools and keeping an accurate count was a chore each day. Supplies of sandpaper, nails, screws, and wood finish were also required. The girls rotated through this training along with the boys. As they cut, planed, fastened, and applied finish they learned basic woodworking skills. It was, at least, an introduction to skills they never considered before.

The plans for vocational classes were developed before the Otino Waa Cafe and Gift Shop were built. Carol designed the cafe kitchen with three student kitchens and a demonstration counter. Each student kitchen was fully equipped with a stove, sink, pots and pans, utensils, and mixing bowls. Three or four students shared each kitchen area as they learned to cook, bake, read a recipe, measure ingredients, and clean up properly. As they gained skills, the food they prepared was sold to customers stopping at the cafe.

They also learned to take orders, make change from the cash box, serve customers with a smile and, in general, be pleasant and attentive to the customers. Students who were quiet and on the shy side found this challenging, but with practice, they became less reserved. The outgoing kids were very engaging and loved the interaction.

Travelers stopping at the Otino Waa Cafe were almost speechless when they saw soft-serve ice cream and cinnamon rolls on the menu. Carol had taught her students to make Blue Ribbon quality cinnamon rolls. They were wonderful, and finding them in remote Northern Uganda was unbelievable! The cooking and catering training was a solid success.

On a rest and relaxation weekend in Jinja, at the source of the Nile River, Carol saw a small container of honey, displayed in a teacup-sized hut. An attached phone number put her in touch with Lester, a Singaporean, who was an expert beekeeper. Some planning and scheduling set up a week-long beekeeping training for about twelve of the Otino Waa staff and older boys. We knew nothing as we started, but by the end of the week, we knew the basics. And we had plans in hand for building our own Kenya Top Bar bee hives. They were a simple design, we could build them ourselves, and they worked.

Soon after, a US church team arrived and helped build our first hives. A remote spot on our property was chosen for the hives to be placed. Then, we waited for swarming bees to find a new home in our hives. And, one by one, the hives were filled with bees.

These were African bees that came with an aggressive attitude!

They were easily agitated and that mood could sweep across the hive in less than a minute. Hundreds of bees would be smacking you from all directions with stingers ready for action.

A bee suit was a must any time the hive was opened to collect honey. But we had no real bee suits, so we improvised. Coveralls were bought in Lira at the used clothes market. Worn over a long sleeve shirt and long pants, gave a double layer of material, which was usually sting resistant. Rubber or leather gloves protected the hands and rubber boots were best for the feet. Rubber bands at wrists and ankles stopped the bees from entering.

The bee veil was the challenge. A brimmed hat, with a stiff wire sewn to the outer edge, held a piece of mosquito netting away from the face. Getting the netting to close the gap at the collar was a problem. A scarf tied at the neck usually worked. But even the smallest gap was an entry point for angry stinging bees. If bees breached the veil there were now bees inside the netting. Stinging bees at your eyes, lips, and nose was terrifying. It came close to a scene from a horror movie! This would unnerve even the most seasoned beekeeper.

Eventually, bees filled our forty hives. The honey they produced was harvested, processed, bottled, and sold in the gift shop. It was top-quality honey and sold well.

Beeswax from the hives was melted down and made into candles. The students were personally involved in all the processes, from hive to packaged honey. Skills were learned. Beekeeping became a major vocational training area and income producer for Otino Waa.

A US visitor suited up with the beekeeping students for an inspection of the hives. This is his account of the experience:

"A dozen of us gathered in the bee center, to armor up. It was time for the weekly inspection of the beehives to see how the well-trained Otino Waa kids handle those famous African 'killer' bees. After suiting up with coveralls, rubber gloves, a veil made from a mosquito net, and a brimmed hat, we walk slowly, a quarter mile, to the apiary. I noticed the netting in my bee veil

Beekeeping was one area of vocational training. The suited up student is holding a beautiful capped honeycomb.

has taken away about 75% of my vision. It's night, so I'm thinking a flashlight could come in handy. I'm wondering how I'll ever be able to run if this all goes south?

"What could go wrong?

"As the bee team carefully opened the hives to check the top bars for honey, it quickly became evident the bees have large ears or spies. They knew we were coming! Within seconds, the bees poured out of each hive frantically, determined to bring down the enemy. No one is given grace. No matter where you stand, how loud your cries, or how well your bee suit fits, all are under attack!

"As interesting as this beekeeping process was, I immediately felt alone and isolated, as the first bees struck my outer defenses. As the hits mounted, a minor panic set in! There was a large angry riot gathered on the netting in front of my face. I could almost hear high-pitched voices saying something like, 'You are mine, you foolish Muzungu.' (Muzungu is the term for white guy.)

"Wait, feel that? That tickle can't be what I think it is. BAM-on the right ankle! Okay, the urge to run has to be put away. BAM-on the left ankle! Slowly back away, but there's definitely something crawling up my leg at a frightening pace. BAM-on the thigh! Slow your breathing down. BAM-on the neck! Where's the gate? BAM-on the ankle again! BAM-on the neck again! How are these guys getting in so fast? My attention is drawn straight ahead. This can't be! There's buzzing in front of my face and adrenaline is now in full flow. Is that guy inside or out? He's in! Now try to keep calm as your fear shouts in your ear, 'Abandon ship!'"

Needless to say, the visit to the apiary made a lasting impression!

Sewing was the next area of vocational training. Carol learned to sew from her mother, and sewing classes in college. She was a trained teacher in sewing and loved to sew. This was an area of her expertise.

She contacted the Janome sewing machine company in Japan and convinced them to donate twelve sewing machines. These machines were brand new high quality, electric machines. Carol's students learned to sew on the finest machines in the region. They learned to straight stitch, hem, zigzag, and back stitch. If they didn't follow directions, the stitch ripper was called to take it apart and sew it again.

They learned to follow patterns, cut fabric, and pin pieces together for proper alignment. There was so much to learn but with much repetition, they remembered. Sewing had immediate income-producing potential.

Agriculture is Uganda's greatest income producer. The climate, soil, and rainfall combine into a winning combination to produce wonderful crops. Arabica coffee, tea, and sugarcane are exported, as well as flowers for the European markets.

Rural farmers, who depend on their crops for subsistence, do well when conditions are right. Maize, cassava, pineapple, millet, and peanuts are produced. But during a drought and during the dry season, seeds fail to sprout, causing food shortages.

Meeting Mike Hafner, a retired John Deere employee, was timely for us. He was in Uganda working on agricultural projects. Carol met Mike in the Otino Waa Cafe one day and was soon urging him to teach an ag class to a group of our secondary students. Teaching ag was not his training, but Carol was very persuasive. Mike had reservations but did agree to start a class. The kids loved him! They really clicked together. It was a fun class.

Mike introduced the concept of drip irrigation. In the dry season drip irrigation could grow much-needed produce with very little water. And it would bring a good price to the market.

Mike followed through by providing the water tanks and plastic pipe for a drip system at Otino Waa. He gave planting instructions

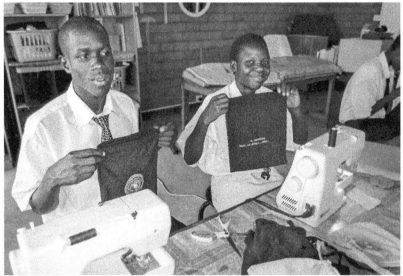

Students hold up a completed sewing project.

and other pertinent information for successful crop production. He taught them farming with drip technology, a higher level of ag. Their first crop of peppers, tomatoes, cabbage, and melons proved it really worked. Mike made it all happen, to our great delight! Vocational agriculture was now a reality in our training program.

The final area of vocational training was computer skills. Our goal was to have thirty working computers, enough for an entire class of students. Donated computers came to us from office upgrades, and individuals wanting to help. Some arrived in the luggage of visiting teams. We had a variety of computer models and different software packages. This was a start, but it was a challenge to teach

"MS Word" when some had open-source software.

Over time, and with the help of knowledgeable computer people, the same software was installed on all the computers. When the teacher gave instruction, it applied to everyone in the room. This was such a help and learning was greatly enhanced.

Typing lessons stressed proper hand placement on the keyboard to teach typing with all ten fingers without looking. The students started to get the hang of it when they practiced with a typing program. They felt they had a real accomplishment when they reached twenty or thirty words per minute. They were really impressed if they looked over Carol's shoulder when she was typing eighty to one hundred words per minute! It drove home the message that typing skills would get your work done much faster and that practice was the key to speed.

All secondary students received computer instruction. Some excelled, as though they were meant for the computer. They just got it. They learned and became good at it. Computer skills could secure a good-paying job wherever they went in Uganda. The computer lab was expensive and required frequent attention to keep it all working, but it was worth the effort. Computers are essential in every business and industry. The computer lab prepared our students to fill those positions if their interests took them there. We are very grateful to the many who made the Otino Waa computer lab the best in all of Northern Uganda.

Upon graduation, some desired to take advanced schooling for nursing, teaching, catering, law, flying, and accounting. A scholarship fund was established and interested graduates could submit an application. Funds were limited so not all requests could be met. Prior grades, behavior, and seriousness as a student, were evaluated before an in-person interview was given, to the delight of some and the disappointment of others.

This gives some insight into the vocational training that helped develop skills that could lead to employment upon graduation. It helped students identify areas they liked or did not like.

We were doing what we could to help the most promising graduates get the advanced schooling they needed. Vocational classes were introductions to job possibilities. The scholarship program took them a step further. Each program stretched our budget and gave us deep pause if we dared commit to more spending. We relied on the Lord's provision.

Agriculture is Uganda's greatest asset. Students are learning drip irrigation which can grow lush crops with minimum water.

>> Chapter 30
BRAIN BLEED

Douglas, our transportation and beekeeping director, missed the weekly staff meeting, reporting as sick. Unusual for him, he was seldom sick. He didn't improve and after several days he was admitted to Lira Hospital. Malaria treatment didn't help. The doctors didn't know what was wrong and he was getting worse. Some left-side paralysis hastened our decision that he needed to be taken to Kampala International Hospital immediately.

I was the obvious choice to drive him there so we left for Kampala directly. His wife, Grace, insisted on going too and she had to take her nursing daughter. I was a bit perplexed wondering how I would deal with seriously ill Douglas, his wife, and a nursing baby.

We arrived after dark and got Douglas admitted, and his condition was serious – left-side paralysis. The doctors conferred and scheduled brain surgery for the first thing in the morning. It couldn't wait. There was actually a neurosurgeon on staff, able to operate. They removed a section of his skull to relieve the pressure against his brain, which was causing the paralysis.

For no apparent reason, he had developed a brain bleed between his skull and brain. Sometimes this is caused by a blow to the head or a fall, but none was true for Douglas. It just happened. Left untreated it could have resulted in death or permanent mobility and speech impairment.

We stayed in the hospital for about a week and he was discharged showing remarkable recovery. Some weeks at home regaining his strength was all he needed. He returned to work with no noticeable problems.

I thought it was great he was okay without realizing it was in the realm of the miraculous. On the next trip home to the US I related the story to Tom Bonn, a physical therapist who was one of our board members. He had patients who suffered the same brain bleed and never recovered fully. He was amazed Douglas had no lingering impairment.

I remember paying the surgeon's bill for the operation. He charged $400! (Outrageous, don't you think, for a neurosurgeon to charge like that?) I wonder what that would have cost in Oregon?

If Douglas had not been on staff at Otino Waa he most likely would have stayed in Lira and not gotten treatment in Kampala. He would not have had surgery and would have died or been permanently disabled, unable to walk or speak clearly. Probably never be able to work again.

It would have been a tragic loss. Douglas was our second most important staff member. He oversaw all transportation for the ministry and beekeeping. He later became pastor of the second church Rev. Dickens started and it thrived under his leadership. Pastor Douglas was Carol's weekly radio program interpreter – their conversation flowed flawlessly over the airwaves, never missing a beat together. He was excellent in every area that he was working in. It would have been a tremendous loss to us if he had died. We were so grateful for the trained doctors at the Kampala hospital which gave treatment that we could not get anywhere else.

A brain bleed sent Douglas to Kampala for life saving surgery.

>> Chapter 31
OTINO WAA SECONDARY SCHOOL

Otino Waa Primary School had been completed for several years and the students were advancing a grade level each year. This resulted in more of our kids entering private secondary schools. We enrolled them in boarding schools in the area and paid their school fees. For a few students, this was okay. But as the number increased, it became evident that we needed to start our own secondary school.

This was another major step. We had enough secondary-age students to capture our attention, but not enough, when compared to the teachers we needed to hire. Secondary school teachers typically taught one subject – like math or history. Even if a teacher was required to teach two subjects, the teacher-to-student ratio was very high. It would take many teachers for a few students, to begin our secondary school.

There was much to consider. An additional school block had to be built for the needed classrooms. More teachers meant more salaries. Textbooks in every subject and grade level were needed.

After much debate, the decision was made. There was a lot to do to be ready for the start of the school year the following February. We decided to start secondary one and two (equivalent to freshman and sophomore) in the first year. The next year, we would add secondary three, then four.

More classrooms were needed when Otino Waa Secondary School was started.

The newly hired secondary headmaster (principal) readied his staff and the first day of classes began. The students took their seats on the new school benches, seated two or three at each new table. The teachers were at their new desks and roll call was the first order of business. As names were called out, there was only silence. Not a single student would speak up. In solidarity, they were boycotting the start of school. They were protesting that textbooks in every subject were not available! Every teacher for every subject was not hired. The first day of school was not perfect in their estimation!

It took but a few minutes for this news to reach Auntie Carol and Rev. Dickens. They assembled all those rebellious students and sat them down for a talk. In previous weeks the students had been well informed of all the preparations being made on their behalf. But not everything could be done at once. Some things take time.

We no longer had to send our secondary students to boarding school. Their focus and study time was improved by staying at Otino Waa.

The students' behavior ignited fury in Auntie Carol and Rev. Dickens. He explained, in glowing terms, that none of them had to be at Otino Waa Secondary School or stay at Otino Waa. They were not held captive in any way. They were there voluntarily. They were free to leave and would be asked to leave if they refused to go to class and participate as respectful students.

There was a long waiting list of those wanting to come to Otino Waa that would gladly take their places. Not one student missed the meaning of this talk. Shall we say, they were sobered? (probably chilled). Every one of them knew their name and could speak it out when they returned to class for roll call.

Getting Otino Waa Secondary School established was a great benefit for our older students. They had the stability of being at Otino Waa, the church across the highway provided a God connection, and their school gave them what they needed for academic achievement. This set the stage for them to thrive. They just needed to stay focused and study to take advantage of all that had been provided to them. After the students adjusted their thinking on that first day, they settled in and the school went on very nicely.

"The plans of the diligent certainly lead to advantage..."
- Proverbs 21:5

>> **Chapter 32**

SCIENCE LAB

The Otino Waa Secondary School was up and running, about to complete its second full year of operation. The first year started with students in Senior One and Two. Equivalent in the US to freshman and sophomore years. The next year, Senior Three was added so the classes could move up a year.

As we planned for the next school year, however, we had a problem. We knew we needed to add Senior Four, but we were out of classrooms. There was no physical place for them to meet. Our options were: 1) Use the church across the highway. The big drawback was having them cross the busy road several times a day. 2) Buy a tent. Tents are hot and not easy to secure. 3) Put up a tarp and meet under a big tree. Nothing about that seemed like a great idea. The Senior Four class also needed a science lab. What to do about this lack of space was very troubling, no good answer was in sight.

As we were trying to think this through, we had a small team from the US come to see Otino Waa for themselves. They had heard us talk about it and they wanted to see it in person. When they arrived they wanted to see everything, so I took them on a walking tour. As we approached the school blocks, I pointed out the section of rooms for the Primary classes and for the Secondary. I explained we had rooms for Senior One, Two, & Three and would be adding Senior Four for the coming year, but we had no classroom. I was just talking through our situation. Milt, one of our guests stopped right there and asked, "What would it cost to build the room you need?"

I wasn't prepared for that question since an actual building had not been drawn. I hadn't considered the possibility of someone paying for the building we needed. The building needed to have a classroom, a science lab (biology, chemistry, physics), teachers' prep and lunch room, and the headmaster's (principal's) office. I knew the building costs from previous buildings, so I could come up with a fairly accurate estimate.

When I told Milt the cost, $36,000, he said, "Let's build it!" Just like that, he committed to finance our much-needed school block. I was left breathless. We absolutely did not have the money to even consider building, so this news was shocking, in a very wonderful way!

Soon Rev. Dickens arranged to take me to visit science labs in several schools in the district. It was good to see examples of what we needed in our science lab.

Now, I was ready to draw plans and start building. Planning the classroom, teachers' room, and headmaster's office was relatively easy, but the science lab took more thought. Multiple lab stations needed sinks, running water, drains, and piping for propane for Bunsen burners. Tile countertops were needed for easy cleaning and durability. The same for the teacher's demonstration table at the front of the class.

The plan came together and was reviewed for final approval. It looked good, so the builders were turned loose with plans in hand. Foundation, slab, and walls appeared. Daily progress was made. Their diligent work produced a lovely building, ready for the start of the next school year. The Senior Four class had a classroom, teachers had their room, the headmaster had his office, and the splendid science room was equipped and ready for biology probing, chemistry test tubes, and physics magnets.

The wonderful science building housed the headmaster's office, teachers room, classroom, and science lab.

I had agonized over a solution to our lack of a classroom for the coming year, with no hint that the answer was on the way. It took a very big step of faith to start Otino Waa Secondary School. It progressed well in the first two years. So for Senior Four to fall into place, was the final piece of school development we needed. We praise God for sending the answer. His timing was perfect!

>> Chapter 33
FAITH OR PRESUMPTION?

Teams from America love to take on a project and see it through to completion. This was very evident, as Circle Three was being built. Circle One and Two were completed and working well. They had gone from idea to concept, to reality. The houses were built, the beds were filled, and the moms were caring for their house full of kids. Meals, school, bathing, and sleep had a daily rhythm. This brought enthusiasm to build the eight houses of Circle Three. Several individuals decided they wanted to finance and help build a house in that circle. They raised the money and a few actually came and helped build the house. The cost at that time was $11,600 per house.

We were blessed to see houses going up. The visiting team was blessed, seeing their house take shape with their own hands. The Otino Waa kids were blessed, seeing more houses going up, knowing that meant more nearly hopeless orphans would have a place to live. It was a marvelous win for everyone. A thrilling time of building and growth and expansion.

The Americans saw the need, it was financially possible, they could help build it, and it could be completed in a few weeks. What a perfect project. And they did it! Seeing their completed house brought satisfaction and fulfillment of an accomplished project.

A US team member helps lay a wall for a Circle Three house.

When the dust cleared, there stood the completed houses. The beds, dining tables, benches, the mom's furniture, and rocket stoves were all in place. They were ready for a house mom, and the eight kids.

But we had a big problem; a troubling situation. This was territory we never encountered before. Yes, we were thrilled to have the new houses the teams had provided. There sat three completed houses with no kids. There were over 100 orphans on the waiting list so there was no lack there. The issue was we had no sponsorship money to support that many new kids.

Our costs were $100 per child per month. That covered food, clothes, school, and supplies. So, three houses of eight make for twenty-four children. Twenty-four times $100 is an additional $2,400 per month. We did not have the income. It just wasn't there.

This was our dilemma. God had provided three houses through generous zealous donors. So, we reasoned, if He had provided the houses, we should take the step of faith and fill the houses. The money wasn't there, but surely He would provide. We would be walking by faith.

We knew once the houses were filled, that cost would be there every coming month. Were we showing a lack of faith by delaying? And those empty house donors were getting agitated with us, for not filling their house.

On the other hand, since the money was not there, it could be presumptuous to move ahead. What if we filled the houses and God was not behind all this? If we got ahead of God and made our own decision, we could be in trouble. If we made the move and God was not providing, in two months we would be about $5,000 in the red. In four months it would be $10,000. The prospect of this playing out was chilling.

Faith or presumption; we had never been this squarely at the crossroads of deciding which path to take. By filling the houses, we could be applauded for our courageous walk of faith. Not walking by sight, but by faith, trusting in God.

By not filling the houses, we could be listed with the, "Oh you of little faith". If God provided the houses, surely He would provide for the children to fill them. Isn't that obvious to you?

The house is taking shape as walls close in on window and door frames.

We talked and prayed. We consulted our board. We waited. We did not have a clear go-ahead, so we waited for months. Eventually, our income increased and we filled a house, then another.

Building a house for eight is a great project. It is affordable and quick. Getting new sponsors to cover the costs of the new orphans is less compelling. It takes a lot of diligence and effort to get the new sponsors.

So, in the end, we were cautious to spend money we did not have. As income increased, we took that as God's go-ahead to fill a house. Walking by faith, but not presumptuously, was a tension-filled time I shall never forget.

>> Chapter 34

FUNDRAISING

When we moved to Uganda it meant we moved away from in-come-producing work. Our house was paid for. We were debt-free, but we needed income to live and meet expenses in Uganda. Fund-raising in Oregon, before our departure to Uganda, started with a letter Carol sent to our Christmas list of friends. It stated our intent to train church leaders in rural Uganda with the video curriculum we had tried out the previous year. That trial run had given us con-fidence that the bilingual format was perfect for Uganda, the con-tent had a profound impact on the untrained rural pastors, and that we could train a lead pastor to direct a school. Our plea was, "Please send money to help us train these willing but untrained pastors." Some responded and the money was banked.

We also sold possessions, like my red Mazda work pickup and lum-ber rack; our small travel trailer, and a toolbox. Carol's Uncle Tom believed in us and gave a very sacrificial gift to support our move.

Not a large amount, but huge in heart. It was greatly appreciated.

Friends and family pitched in; however, we lacked the backing of any specific local church. Church sponsorship would have added stability to us, but it didn't happen that way. We were truly independent missionaries. We bought plane tickets and headed to Uganda with four 70 lb boxes of possessions and cash in our money pouches hidden under our clothes. Once in Uganda, we were glad to get that cash banked.

There was a cost for everything we did. We had house rent; a bit

of house furniture to buy; a town taxi; and travel to three ISOM schools that were launched. The schools needed generators, TVs for monitors, microphones, and speakers. And, of course, we had to eat. We did all we could until we were out of money. So we boarded British Airways with the other half of our round-trip tickets and headed back home. We had only been in Uganda for six months.

Bringing a report to my boyhood church in Burns, Oregon was a joyous fundraising event. Many old-time friends there.

We needed to raise funds to resume the pastor training. We told our limited story to individuals, to church small groups, and to every local church that would open their doors to us. Carol wrote a newsletter to share our story with a wider audience.

Enough money came in for us to buy plane tickets and support us in Uganda for a while longer. Fundraising was a whole new endeavor for us and we didn't know exactly how to do it. Starting out we lacked credibility.

1) We were too old. At 55 years old what mission board would choose to send us?

2) We had no mission training. No cross-cultural training; no language skills; no travel experience.

3) We had no track record. No other mission projects to prove our suitability.

4) We were underfunded. That is totally understated. There was no foundation, mission organization, trust fund, wealthy person, or large church having our back.

5) We had no Bible school training. Being Christians for years was our training.

Nothing about our situation would impress anyone with thoughts about our likely success. As I said, we lacked credibility! Under these circumstances, it was difficult to fundraise. It was mostly friends and family that gave because they loved us. Meager funds were spent very sparingly on essentials only. We were surviving, but barely.

As we responded to the needs we saw, other projects were started. The fact that we were in Uganda for several years training pastors; had completed several water projects; and were providing minor medical care, built our credibility. Donors had more confidence that their gifts would be well spent on projects they believed in. People, other than friends and family, began to support and income was increasing.

A Bible verse in James states, "You have not, because you ask not." Our approach was to ask God and ask people. Asking people, especially Christians, to give and support God-centered projects seemed a reasonable ask. How can someone give, if there is no knowledge of a need? Willing givers may just need to be informed.

As an example: Carol sent an email describing how improving a spring could provide clean water for hundreds, possibly thousands of people, for just $1,000. People eagerly gave for such a great project, once they heard.

People were informed of our activities with newsletters, emails, in-person reports to US churches, talking with individuals, and giving church small group presentations. We put on fundraising dinners. Over time we developed connections to churches in Washington and California, as well as Oregon. A sponsorship program was started to care for orphans.

We held very strongly to the principle of God's provision being an indicator of ministry direction. If the money was there, we would move ahead. If it wasn't, we did not proceed.

This example is clear in my memory. The ISOM schools were thriving in Uganda, Rwanda, and a few in Congo. Sudan was asking and there was a start-up in Tanzania.

Carol shared in a newsletter that there was interest from a group of pastors in Ethiopia. We were prepared to start school there. The first ISOM book was already translated into Amharic by an Ethiopian in Kampala. We waited for the response from the newsletter: and we waited and waited. I was shocked, even dismayed by the absolute lack of any financial support. Not $1 came in.

For us that was a halt to going to Ethiopia. The leg work was done. We were ready and willing but no funds confirmed going there. We took it as God shutting the door by not supplying the funds.

Financial accountability was important to us, to God, to our board, and to donors in the US. It was an ongoing priority to guard against the deep-seated corruption that gripped the country. We saw ourselves as stewards of the money entrusted to us for the ministry in Uganda. We wanted to assure our donors their money was handled properly and used where needed. An offended donor is lost forever.

To illustrate, Carol's mother gave money to Jimmy to buy bicycles for his children. He was visiting the US and was our Ugandan guest for a few days. But when he returned home he spent the bicycle money on a pickup he needed. When that news reached Carol's mother she never gave another dollar. Her heartfelt donation had been misspent and she was offended. Handling donors' dollars with accuracy and transparency is so essential.

We went to Uganda with almost nothing. We worked hard; reported our doings and, bit by bit, a wider giving audience gained confidence in what we were doing and added their support. Our meager beginning took root and grew into more than we ever imagined possible. This motto became a dominant theme for us:

Do what you can,

With what you have,

Where you are.

It seemed to fit our experience precisely. It guided our humble start, our uncertain growth, and each new project. We worked, people gave, and God directed. Our budget grew to almost $1,000,000. No one was more amazed than we were!

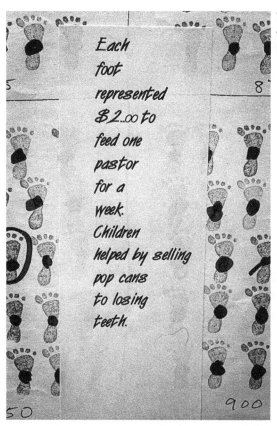

Each foot represented $2.00 to feed one pastor for a week. Children helped by selling pop cans to losing teeth.

These funds sponsored the ISOM pastor training in Arua, Uganda.

Chapter 35

A NEAR RIOT, AND A SIMPLE NAPKIN

My dear wife Carol certainly didn't mean to cause such a serious situation. She could not have known the excitement that a simple radio announcement would create. On a Tuesday morning in September, Carol made a quick announcement at the end of her broadcast. "This week on Thursday, Friday, and Saturday, we will be having a medical and dental clinic at the Ilera Church and Otino Waa Children's Village, it will be led by American doctors from a church in California."

That was all that Carol had said. But that Thursday, in the early morning hours of darkness, villagers were already walking down long dirt paths or riding their bikes along the rural roads that fanned out around Otino Waa. Some carried needy children on their backs, and others pedaled, with elderly loved ones on the back of their bicycles. By sunup, the night watchmen at Otino Waa were supervising a long line of people along the roadside. By 8:00

a.m., when the clinic opened, the crowd at our rural location was almost out of hand. Earlier, Pastors Cliff and Mari Hanes assisted, as Dr. John Roberts and dentist, Dr. Mark Nadler, carefully set up their supplies. Dr. John would be seeing patients in the tiny storeroom of the Ilera Church, and Dr. Mark, with his wife Debbie, would be treating dental patients in the office library.

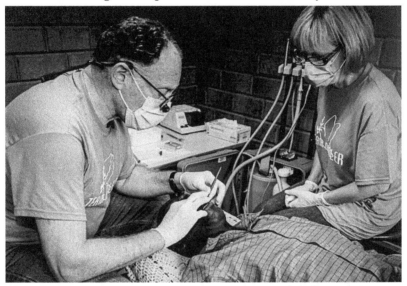

Chaise lounge dentistry at Otino Waa in the expert hands of Dr. Mark Nadler assisted by wife Debbie.

But, as the unexpected crowds needing a doctor grew, the team had to spring into action. Long tables were set up in front of the church as barriers, and these tables were manned by team members. They were tasked with dispensing medicines; aspirin and vitamins, deworming tablets, antibiotic ointment, and stronger medicines that the doctor would prescribe.

A triage nurse began to walk among the long line of people giving out green tickets to those who needed urgent help, and blue tickets for those who could see a nurse for advice and prescriptions. As many patients as the wooden benches of the church could hold were allowed into the church. Cliff and Mari and Carol spent a long day of crowd control. At one point, Carol stood on a chair shouting, "Calm, please! No pushing!"

Meanwhile, Dr. Mark and his wife Debbie worked in the heat of their makeshift dental office. Dr. Mark came with a suitcase-sized portable dental unit. It was equipped with everything! It drilled, it suctioned, it was amazing! We rounded up a plastic chaise lounge as our dental chair, Dr. Mark strapped on a hikers headlamp, the generator was fired up, and the first young patient was brought in.

Before the team arrived, we surveyed all the children to see who had dental issues. The setup was primitive but Dr. Mark and Debbie made it work; they drilled, filled, scraped, and polished. As the list of needy students grew shorter, they were able to address the needs of the house mothers and other staff members as well.

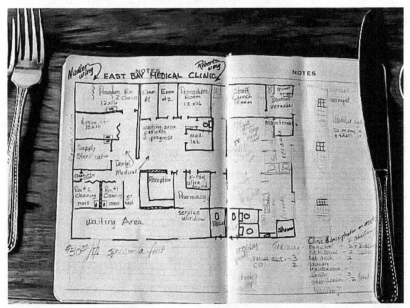

The dream of a clinic at Otino Waa was sketched out as Dr. Nadler and Dr. Roberts brainstormed with Carol over dinner at Paara Lodge.

On the third day, they were even able to see children who had arrived on a bus from an orphanage in another village! And everyone, all the children of Otino Waa, the visitors, and even all the people who lined up for the medical clinic at the church, were given dental hygiene kits with toothbrushes, toothpaste, soap, and other items.

These days of dental care were unprecedented for us. In rural Uganda, oral hygiene and dental care were almost non-existent. A person would wait until their tooth hurt so bad that it had to be pulled, not fixed. What would become an ongoing dental office at Otino Waa was "hatched" that week.

After those long days of hard work and the Sunday Services of rejoicing with our students and staff and the team, a night and day of rest was scheduled for the team at Paraa Lodge at Murchison Falls National Park. Getting to see hippos and elephants on the Nile River boat ride, seeing bounding antelope on the grasslands, watching graceful giraffes stretching their necks to graze from treetops - this was a relaxing end to a very intense medical time at Otino Waa.

During the evening meal on the lodge's veranda, Carol and Dr. Mark, and Dr. John were engaged in conversation about the obvious need for a medical and dental clinic at Otino Waa. Carol was fully engaged and ideas were flowing. She spread out a paper napkin from the table and sketched out a clinic design that might work. The next morning at breakfast, this design was copied into pages of Dr. John's notebook. The team talked about what the cost of this building might be. From that napkin design came the core concept of a clinic that might one day be possible. Rooms for medical, dental, pharmacy, lab, and limited surgical procedures. Even birthing for the community.

The idea so resonated with the team that they ran with it that fall when they returned home. Dr. Mark fundraised from his office to whoever would lend an ear. Dr. John and other team members shared at spaghetti dinners and the church's retreats in-home group gatherings. At Christmas time, Pastor Cliff announced a special offering would be taken. After the Christmas Eve service there was great rejoicing, the goal of $50,000 had been reached!

Pastor Cliff Hanes, Dr. Mark Nadler, and Dr. John Roberts carried the vision for a clinic at Otino Waa back to the US and fundraised into a reality.

The following month, Pastor Mari called Carol to say that the entire amount was now available to build the clinic. We were stunned and filled with absolute joy! Carol, the idea lady, had proposed the clinic during a "hoping it might happen someday" brainstorming supper. What a thrill to go from, "Wouldn't this be wonderful" to "The money is in the bank", and all this in a matter of months!

The hasty sketch over dinner at Paraa Lodge got the ball rolling.

Now it was time to get a serious drawing done so the builders could start. "What did I know about designing a clinic?" Not much, that was for sure. With t-square and triangles, I got some lines on the first draft. I had questions. What room size does a dentist need? What size of the medical exam room? How can there be privacy and windows? How can the clinic be situated to be community-friendly and Otino Waa-friendly?

I had doctor friends in Uganda and the US critique the plans. They pointed out flaws so I drew again. And again. And again. By the fifth try, I finally had their approval. The room size, hall width, sink locations, check-in and check-out properly placed, and waiting area out of the sun, all seemed to fit. The pharmacy had security bars and a steel door to prevent theft. We checked the plans again for lighting, ventilation, security, flow of patient care, and adequate storage of equipment and supplies. It was time to call in the masons.

The clinic was our finest building. The floors were tiled. The hall ceiling was made from split bamboo. There was running water in each treatment room. Gutters were installed to deliver rainwater to a water tank for outside patient hand washing. A fridge was bought to keep sensitive meds cool and an inside flushing toilet was there for the staff.

Carol painted the partition columns with an African motif and hung clinic-themed pictures in blank spaces – pictures painted by Lira artist, Isaac Okwir. All the planning paid off. The clinic was organized, functional, well-equipped, and beautiful to behold. Dr. Mark, Dr. John, and Carol birthed a vision, a host of workers constructed it and brought forth the top-class Otino Waa Clinic.

The clinic had two dental rooms, two medical treatment rooms, a lab, an office, a pharmacy, and intake and check-out windows. It was of sufficient size to accommodate many patients without crowding. The Bible declares that without a vision the people perish. Without Carol's clinic vision people would have continued to suffer toothache and medical needs. Expert medical and dental care was now available at the new clinic. From vision to the completed clinic in less than a year was truly amazing!

Chapter 36

PRISON ART

My sister, Jane, was married to Steve Brabb the prison chaplain at the Snake River Prison in Ontario, Oregon. Carol and I were visiting them, while home from Uganda, and Steve invited us to go with them to the prison for a chapel service.

Otino Waa had been in operation for a couple of years and we had been talking with them about it. Steve thought the inmates would have an interest in an African orphan project so he asked us to share for a few minutes in the service. That small introduction was the beginning of all that was to follow.

Through later visits we learned the inmates created artwork; some woodworking; some drawing and some painting. Ideas about inmate art and orphans were churning and soon a plan was hatched. Steve talked to the warden, seeking permission on several levels: 1) Could the prisoner art leave the prison? 2) Could it be sold?

3) Could the income from the sales be used to support orphans in Uganda?

Prisons have rules and they're very careful that nothing is illegal or a scam in any way. Their investigation found everything to be legitimate and Steve was allowed to receive the artwork. We could then display it for sale with all proceeds designated for Otino Waa. None of us were making any money from the efforts of the inmates.

Exquisite inmate art, when sold, supported orphan children at Otino Waa.

What a connection this was! Inmates were supporting orphans. Having a purpose in life sprang from their talent having an outlet. They painted, sketched, drew, and wood burned and others bought the labor of their hands. Off the money went, to buy an orphan a shirt, a supper of fish and rice, or a notebook and pen for school.

Prisoners with no direction or purpose now had a way to help orphans in Uganda. These orphans had faced a future with no hope in sight. Before Otino Waa they had no hope of attending school, having enough to eat, or being loved and cared for. Many inmates could identify with feelings of hopelessness so the possibility of bringing hope to an orphan changed their whole outlook. Hopeless prisoner helping homeless orphan.

In 2009, after many pleas from the inmates at Snake River, Dale and Sandy Russell (PATH-US Director and his wife) traveled to the prison to present a basic overview of the progress at Otino Waa. At first, they were reluctant to visit the prison, but that soon disappeared when they actually talked with the inmates who were eager to hear.

By 2012 a customized sponsorship program was introduced to the prison in which they could have a direct connection to one or more of the Otino Waa kids. For $5/month they could sponsor a child which provided them with a biography and photo of their child. They could also exchange letters and send small gifts. A generous donor matched their gift each month. What a dynamic connection! I think it is fair to say this fundraising niche is unique. I know of no others like it. This story was the inspiration for a documentary titled, "Lost and Found". (See Epilogue for details on this film).

It reminds me of Jesus watching people as they put their offerings in the temple collection box. A widow putting in a few cents was praised for she had sacrificially given her all. The amount given by the inmates may be small, but compared to their income, it is huge.

This prison outreach eventually became an independent ministry called "Visions of Hope." Led by Dale and Sandy Russell, it is now offered in seven Oregon state prisons. The Russells bring chapel services that inspire and encourage men and women to have faith in God. They include updates from Otino Waa and news from the orphans. It is an outstanding ministry to orphans and inmates. Who would have thought inmates and orphans would have life-changing connections?

This is a brief excerpt from a letter sent from a prison inmate to the sponsored child at Otino Waa:

"I will close for now and just want you to know I am proud of you and all the hard work you are doing. I love hearing from you and to hear you quote the Bible makes me know you are reading daily. That is so good. Tell your friends hello and thank you for the prayers. God bless and keep you in the name of Jesus."
"Love always."

The Otino Waa child replies:

"I would love to thank the Almighty Father for protecting the both of us till now.... Again, I want to remind you to read your Bible and pray every day because God is our protector and our helper. He can protect our lives against the enemy.... I am always praying for all of you so that God should protect your lives and keep on adding you more blessings and more years to live in this world. All my friends have sent the greetings to you and they are also praying for you. May the God of Heaven bless you. Amen. Thanks!"

Inmate art talent produced a wide variety of pictures, suiting many tastes.

The artists became more inspired. Truly motivated. They produced more and more art to sell. Pictures were posted online, displayed in offices, and featured at fundraising dinners. The results of this prison endeavor are quite amazing. About ninety inmates, from prisons across the state, are producing artwork to sell for orphan support. One-third of the orphans at Otino Waa have an inmate sponsor. Art sales and sponsorships have produced over $194,000! All of it was sent directly to Otino Waa!

>> Chapter 37

MARRIAGE BONDING

Moving to Uganda took our marriage relationship to a different level than we previously knew. Before Uganda, Carol and I had a strong tie to each other and worked well together. There were no troublesome unresolved issues. Not to say that my man-mind and her woman-mind were always in total agreement. Marriage does take effort to make it all work.

We found our reliance on each other was way more pronounced, being in a new culture. We were the minority and isolated from our familiar circumstances. In the village, no one spoke English. There were only pit latrines, and no shower or running water. This departure from life as we knew it threw us off stride. So we relied on each other for stability as we faced all the newness.

It was difficult for me to adjust to all the newness. Using a taxi for transportation, open-air markets for food, different languages, and paying in schillings instead of dollars. I felt lost as I wandered the streets of Kampala. My stomach was in knots for weeks on end. I had never experienced such anxiety!

Well, almost never. Once, when returning to Uganda after a visit home, a thunderstorm prevented our landing in Newark. The storm passed, but we missed our connecting flight to Amsterdam. After a night in a hotel, we were back at the airport ticket window but the agent couldn't find our previous booking, so couldn't get us on a flight. I was super stressed, but they figured it out and eventually, we arrived late in Amsterdam. But, too late for that day's flight to Entebbe. We needed another room, a taxi, and food! I was a stressed-out mess!

We had a day to fill in Amsterdam until the next flight, so we booked a tour bus of the city, but I was lost on the sidewalk. No one spoke English to help me find the bus! My brain was shutting down from the overwhelming accumulated stress. That's when Carol stepped in with her unruffled calmness and saved the day.

It was evident I do better with a plan, a schedule, and knowing how a situation will play out. I got better with time. I got used to all the newness of life in Uganda and I got my bearings. Then I was okay, I could function normally.

Carol, on the other hand, was a much better pioneer. She could go into the unknown and tackle whatever happened. Not a problem for her. We helped each other, relied on each other, and realized we needed each other's strengths to cover the other's weaknesses.

Carol was quick and impulsive and would get frustrated when

people or projects moved slower than she liked. I tended towards steady and methodical. We were a balance for each other. And we found life in Uganda magnified stressful situations that pushed our irritable buttons.

Supporting each other through stress and bliss kept us going week by week.

I found this page in Carol's journal which gives some insight into the stresses we faced.

I have malaria--the third time in nine weeks.

The dog has mange.

The house in Lira is infested with mosquitoes, it needs to be fumigated.

A boy ran into the side of the car as our driver was traveling on the highway-boy died.

The car is wrecked.

The car is impounded with the police 150 miles from town.

The internet isn't working.

The tech now made it so our computer doesn't work at all.

We have two surgery patients to care for.

Our friend Pastor Fred was brutally murdered.

When issues like this multiply, it can be overwhelming! Stress on many fronts.

Our years in Uganda actually brought stronger bonding to our marriage. With each new struggle, we relied on each other more. We knew we could count on the other's support. God blessed us with a love for each other that sustained us through the most difficult of times, emotionally as well as physically. No one knew better what we needed than we did.

Let me state the obvious. We were married, we were bonded like never before, and we were often very stressed. What we needed was marriage intimacy (sex). This topic doesn't get much coverage but it should not be overlooked. It deepens the bonding, is the ultimate stress reliever, and satisfies longings that could get you in trouble. It tames a wandering eye and brings joy and levity in tough circumstances. It can momentarily clear a troubled mind, induce needed sleep, and reset your outlook.

And it is Biblical. The Bible says a husband should love his wife. There you have it. It also says it is not good for man to be alone. Right on. Not alone but together with his wife- do I need to explain? It also says the husband should not deprive his wife, and the wife should not deprive her husband. Deprived of what? You guessed it. The ultimate togetherness.

Every good missionary is intent on serving God, obeying every command and precept. So, it would be disobedient and dishonororing to God if you neglected missionary sexuality. And you need to have frequent fun, to ward off being burned out. Staying healthy and refreshed will prolong fruitful years of ministry.

Struggles and stresses can cause grumpiness in missionaries. If this malady overtakes you, and it can, do not let it dominate your mood all week. The cure really does work and the fun factor is over the top. The cure is the husband together with wife, tonic, God ordained.

Every missionary couple should pay attention to the pressures and stresses they face. To be effective you need physical health, emotional stability, and engaged sexuality. This will enable you to face all sorts of challenges and come out on top.

"The wife does not have authority over her own body, but the husband does; and likewise the husband also does not have authority over his own body, but the wife does."
- 1 Corinthians 7:4

>> Chapter 38
ONE THING LEADS TO ANOTHER

Peacemaker Ministries is a Christian organization, based in the US, that specializes in training people in conflict resolution. Carol had attended several conferences and passed through several stages of training. Through them, she had access to training resources designed for youth.

The orphaned children of Otino Waa were the result of violent conflict in Northern Uganda. The whole region was in turmoil, to the extent that the Ugandan Army and UN forces were heavily involved. Some horrific events even made international news. We were in the zone of armed conflict!

With that background, Carol saw Otino Waa as a perfect host to sponsor a conference for high school-aged kids, themed around conflict resolution. Neighboring schools in the district were invited for a three-day event. Our older students led discussion groups and enacted skits depicting various conflicts. The situations of the skits were discussed and resolution concepts were applied. The conference program was a lot to prepare for, as well as housing and feeding the three hundred visiting attendees. It was an outstanding conference and a huge success!

A reporter from a local radio station in Lira attended one of the training sessions. After hearing Carol speak, he asked if she could be a guest speaker on his radio program. The regular presenter was not available and he wanted her to fill in for the hour.

Carol agreed, and after the hectic weekend conference, the following Tuesday morning, at 5:45, she was in the broadcast studio, Voice of Lango 88.0, with Pastor Douglas as her interpreter. Hers was a new voice, heard that morning, as people prepared for a new day. Without hesitation, she talked of current events and tied scripture verses to the topic. Daily life and Bible were wrapped together as one package. Pastor Douglas spoke Luo and Carol spoke English. Their presentation was smooth, as one voice, but bilingual. It flowed so well, there was no distraction or loss of thought. The hour ended with fifteen minutes of call-in, for questions or comments. There was much listener feedback. "This woman in the morning is very different to listen to." She made that early hour program engaging and it always had a God perspective. They liked hearing the new voice of Auntie Carol and Carol was hooked! She loved it!

Her fill-in status became a request to become a weekly regular. She readily agreed and was on the air every Tuesday morning for five years. Her distinctive voice soon became known to a wide listener audience. One day, we were in a local shop picking up supplies when a woman standing behind us said, "Oh, you're Auntie Carol." She recognized her voice but had never seen her. Carol had become a local radio personality!

A weekly radio program was never even dreamed of, Carol loved it, her listeners tuned in without fail.

Carol always gave them something to think about; often challenging, or at least, an interesting perspective. One topic she spent several weeks exploring was seeing a doctor sooner, not later. She pointed out the risk of hoping a sick baby would get better, so the small expense of medication could be avoided. Doctoring was very cheap, compared to the cost of a funeral, if the baby died. They knew she was right on target, because they saw babies dying way too often, and it was preventable. Carol was not bashful. She spoke boldly addressing sensitive community issues. As a white woman, an outsider, but a resident, she had the freedom to address some issues others avoided. She had earned their respect. They listened to her not wanting to miss any Tuesday.

This was a slice of ministry we could not have anticipated. Carol had followed God's prompting to put on the conference and that drew in the reporter. One thing led to the next, it happened like that often. Completely unexpected, she ended up speaking, on the air, to eager listeners. The radio station found they had someone special, one-of-a-kind, drawing a huge audience tuning in to their station. They estimated Auntie Carol's early morning broadcast reached 700,000 listeners. The number staggered me. What an outreach! My missionary wife said yes, for the initial one-hour fill-in broadcast. It opened for her, years of broadcasting to a host of listeners. She said yes.

What a yes it turned out to be!

"...Just as it is written: "How beautiful are the feet of those who bring good news of good things!"
- Romans 11:15

>> Chapter 39
THE DANGERS WE FACED

In our fourteen years in Africa, we experienced danger from many sources. Not from wildlife, as one might imagine, but mostly on the highway, just going about our usual business. Town traffic moves slowly enough that deadly accidents are usually avoided. The open road is a different story. Roads are often narrow and poorly maintained. Big buses traveled between towns and usually drove too fast. Quick reaction and defensive steering meant survival, as an approaching bus would straddle the centerline.

On a trip, with five of us in the Pajero, without warning a bus overtook us from behind. When I glanced to the side, all I could see was the white side of the bus, an inch from the window. Actually less than an inch, he was in contact with us. Sideswiped, but still upright, we came to a stop in disbelief of what had just happened.

When we traveled between Lira and Kampala, a four or five-hour drive, we often met traffic filling both lanes. Too often it was a bus or taxi passing blindly, rapidly closing the gap which reeked of death. We had a Toyota Land Cruiser VX which turned out to be a lifesaver. It all happened very fast. No traffic was in sight. We had a clear road when suddenly, vehicles in both lanes were coming at us fast. Jerking the wheel hard to the left took us off the road. They flashed past, then we were back up on the road with everything intact. Maybe two or three seconds between death and destruction and down the road we go!

When a regular car or van left the road, to avoid a head-on collision, they usually rolled. Their suspension wasn't designed to handle such a radical maneuver. They avoided the head-on but many died as they rolled and crashed. The beauty of the Land Cruiser was its stability with any off-road maneuver. Not on every trip to Kampala were we forced off the road, but it was frequent. The Land Cruiser saved us on many trips. It may sound a bit too dramatic, to say it saved our life multiple times, but if anything, that is an understatement. That Land Cruiser was a lifesaver!

Another close call was in Congo. We were returning to Kampala after working on a school start-up. We could see a big truck and trailer coming toward us around a sweeping curve. To give him a wide berth, we pulled off onto the shoulder to let him pass. Parked there, we could see him coming, and coming, and he kept coming. Maybe he was sleepy, or mesmerized by hours of driving, or he just didn't focus and see us on the side of the road. He was swinging wide around the outside corner and as he drew ever closer, all that filled our entire view was the truck grill. Flashing across our minds was, "This is it, we're going to die!"

He must have finally seen us because he swerved at the last moment. That massive truck and trailer missed our front corner by about six inches. We had to collect ourselves to make sure we were still alive. We sat trembling, allowing our pounding hearts to slow, and then thankful to be alive, we continued our trip and arrived home safely.

We encountered other potential dangers. No harm came to us, but it could have. There was an Ebola outbreak about thirty miles from us. It was serious enough for the World Health Organization (WHO) to send in its experts. The Ugandan doctors and nurses treating these highly contagious patients were at high risk. They lacked rubber gloves, face masks, and proper scrubs and were trying to care for people that were bleeding. Ebola is a hemorrhaging disease.

It wasn't the worst strain, but serious enough that 30% of those infected died. We took general precautions of less physical contact with people and we stopped getting chicken on a stick from the roadside vendors. WHO intervened and contained the spread of the dreaded disease.

Another potential danger arose as our team was scouting out a location for a medical clinic. The driver asked several townspeople if the drive to the next town was safe. They assured him it was safe, no problem. The safety issue concerned the location of the LRA rebels, who were known to be in that general area.

We had only gone a few miles when we realized there was no one walking along the roadside. This was alarming because there were always people walking, whenever driving along a rural road. Not a soul was in sight. I had never seen an empty rural road.

Then we spotted an occasional man, high up in a tree. Tension in the van was growing by the minute. No one was talking. To the Ugandans, the message was clear. No one walking meant they were all holed up at home, hiding from the rebels. The guys in the trees were rebel spotters keeping close surveillance on all road activity. We were not stopped. We arrived safely at the next town. That tense ride was the closest I came to possibly being shot or abducted. It was a huge relief to again see people walking along the road. The spotters may have been able to see our fearsome guardian angels and decided to leave us strictly alone! Wanting no part of a fight with the likes of them.

Another dangerous encounter occurred while we were returning to Lira from Kampala with a load of supplies for Otino Waa. Carol was in the lead, driving the Pajero, and I was following in the van. We were just leaving a small town, starting to increase to highway speed, when suddenly a bicyclist pulled out directly in front of me. By reflex, I pulled hard to the right to avoid hitting him. When the tires bit into the soft shoulder, the van rolled. Over I went, a complete rotation plus a quarter. I was left hanging from my seat belt. I mentally took body inventory, to see if any part of me was broken.

Quickly a crowd gathered and a few were eager to get me out. I struggled to get turned to get a foot under me before they released my seat belt. I could easily exit through the front window since all the van glass was broken and gone. I was not bleeding or broken. Somehow, I still had my phone and gave Carol a call to come back. "Turn around I've had an accident." When she arrived a few minutes later, she was shocked to see the van on its side. As she rushed over, I assured her I was all right, to her relief.

The van was full of supplies, all the windows were broken, and the crowd that gathered seized the opportunity to help themselves and took whatever they could grab of our cargo. I watched, still a bit dazed, but Carol rushed in with fury. She saw them stealing supplies meant for their orphans and she was incensed. She was shouting and grabbing to retrieve the items they had taken. Loudly, she was pushing looters away from the wheels-in-the-air van. It was intense and chaotic. Finally, a man emerged from the crowd to help Carol. He persuaded her he was there to help. He was on her side and he was a Christian. They held the crowd at bay, to stop any more looting.

I had missed the bicyclist but he crashed and was hurt. The van was secured, so Carol loaded up the injured cyclist and took him back up the road to the nearest hospital. Upon arrival, she found no one there to help, so she gurney-ed him in by herself. The doctor was not there. Imagine that? A hospital with no doctor! Carol was able to locate him and had to bring him to the hospital too!

There were dangers while driving, danger from disease, and danger from violent rebels. Our house was robbed twice, the office safe was beat open and robbed by our guard, our big dog was poisoned, and an out of control driver crashed through our compound wall. Many a crisis! God's hand of protection kept us safe and able to work and stay in Uganda. Without Heavenly help, we would have been sunk. Thank you, Lord!

"...we are afflicted in every way, but not crushed; perplexed, but not despairing; persecuted, but not abandoned; struck down, but not destroyed..." - 2 Corinthians 4:8-9

>> Chapter 40
LEAVING UGANDA

When I turned sixty-eight I started thinking about retirement. The Psalms point out we have seventy years, perhaps eighty. I realized this was not an absolute, but it gave me a reference point in my consideration of the future. A lot was going on with Otino Waa and I was getting tired. It was a lot of work. So I shared with the board my intentions of retiring in two years and that searching for a replacement director was in order. Over time, several prospects were considered and a selection was made. When we moved away the new director would be ready to step in.

In my mind, I was settled about the timeline for leaving Uganda, but Carol was not. She was very engaged with teaching the vocational students, making sure the two cafes were running smoothly, and the two gift shops were stocked and displayed with style. She was very busy and productive.

One morning as she was driving from Lira to Otino Waa the Lord spoke to her a very brief message. "You have done enough." That was it. Only a few words. Not a lengthy message. Those few words were brief but spoke volumes to her heart. It was a release for her, to be able to step away from all the activity, all the responsibilities, all that she had poured her life into for fourteen years. Up to this point, she was not ready to leave. She was holding on, staying fully engaged. Those few words changed everything. It was as though a switch was flipped. She felt mentally and emotionally released and in that brief encounter, her whole outlook changed.

Carol had a very distinct inborn personality. Her approach to life was all in or nothing. Wholeheartedness was the only way she knew how to respond. So when the, "You have done enough", sunk in, and she embraced it, she was ready to leave. She was ready to pack up and leave that week. It was over and she was impatient with the wait, which was necessary for our transition. We needed to go from being in charge to walking away.

Our departure date was set for the last of August 2013. That was also the tenth-anniversary date for Otino Waa, so Carol started planning a big celebration. It was to be a celebration of our fourteen years in Uganda and of Otino Waa being in operation for ten years. Excitement was running high. Much planning was underway for the purchase and preparation of the food it would take to feed the seven hundred anticipated attendees. Invitations were prepared for government officials, alumni, builders, and all the staff. Groups of Otino Waa kids were rehearsing their music, hoping the audition committee would select their group as part of the entertainment. The program was in order with MC, guest speakers, dancing, and singing. The many weeks of preparation brought it all together, as the date approached.

Son Matt, and two of his children, Meagan and Caleb, flew to Uganda, to help us with our move back to the US. It was a delight to have them come and we wanted to make the most of their time with us. We picked them up at the Entebbe airport and drove a couple of hours to where the highway crossed the Equator. There had to be a picture of one foot in the Northern Hemisphere and one in the Southern. Then on to the Kingfisher Resort in Jinja. It is a lovely spot on Lake Victoria at the source of the Nile. We traveled back to Kampala and before leaving town stopped at Garden City Mall.

A little sight-seeing as our son Matt and two kids (Meagan and Caleb) came to give us a hand as we moved back to Bend, Oregon.

After seeing the mall, and lunch, we returned to our car – our broken-into car. Thieves had taken laptops, a camera bag, and worst of all, passports! What a sickening feeling. Robbed in broad daylight, in the open mall lot, with people everywhere and no one saw anything.

We all had tickets to fly home in four days, so it was a frantic scramble to get temporary passports issued by the Embassy, in time for the flight. Caleb needed a signed document from the US to get his approval. Urgent phone calls were complicated by the eleven-hour time difference between Uganda and the US. Tension was high, with phone calls, fax messages, and trips to the Embassy seeking the required passports. They came through on time, but just barely.

Murchison Falls National Park was a planned overnight stop, on the way from Kampala to Lira. A much-needed break from the stress of the previous days and the last stop before final packing. The boat ride on the Nile took us by hippos, (lots of them), crocodiles, diving Kingfishers, then into the churning current just below Murchison Falls.

An overland game drive through the park brought kob, warthog, giraffe, elephant, and cape buffalo up close, for an easy photo shoot. That night, we enjoyed a wonderful buffet at the lodge restaurant. It was a great day of African safari. Then my phone rang.

It was Rory Frink, the new Otino Waa director calling from Lira. His news was shocking. I listened in disbelief. An Otino Waa boy, who was healthy and fine that morning, was now dead. In half a day he had died of a hemorrhaging disease. He bled to death. Not many diseases are in that category and they are usually very contagious and deadly.

Anyone who had been in contact with him was at high risk. Those giving him initial care, those who transported him to the hospital, and the nurses and doctors at the hospital, were all at risk.

The timing of this was gut-wrenching. We had a plane to catch. We could not enter Otino Waa to even say goodbye to our staff, all the children, all those most precious to us. nor could we attend the final Sunday service, for a final farewell there. Meagan and Caleb could not enter Otino Waa to greet any friends they had made on previous visits. We just had to load up and drive out of town with no hugs or goodbyes.

We got to the airport, checked our many bags, and waited in somber silence for the midnight flight back to the US. It was supposed to have been a joyous end to our years in Uganda. The planned party; interaction with the hundreds we had invested our life with; family coming halfway around the world to be with us and help us, all culminating in joy and smiles and our hearts warmed by the expressed love. But it did not happen that way. There was no joy. Our emotions were raw. It was a terrible ending. We left in a dark storm, not the bright of day, as planned. Some situations in life cannot be explained. Why did this happen? Why the tragic end to our story in Uganda?

Little did we realize what the Lord was about to show us all. There was more to be looked at than a celebration of the past. The events of that week can best be described in the words of Rev. Dickens who lived through those days:

"The preparations for the celebration of Bob and Carol's ministry in Uganda were almost completed. The final morning before the Higgins were to return with their visiting family, the Otino Waa children of all ages were involved in the dress rehearsal. All around the orphan houses groups met in full costume to run through their drumming and traditional dances.

An arial view of Otino Waa with Ilera Church across the highway.

Other groups gathered in circles to practice their songs. Finally, the children and house mothers and teachers and staff began to take their places in the long long lineup of several hundred people to practice the festive parade around the grounds that would usher Bob and Carol to their seats in the Pavilion of honor.

"One of the little boys was named Opio Joshua. He was 8 or 9 years old, but very small, and he had only been at Otino Waa for a few months. He stepped away from the parade lineup and went to speak to Pam Frink, the wife of our new director. "Please mum may I sit for a while - I feel a bit tired." Pam took his hand and led him to a place where he could rest in the shade.

"At noon Joshua joined eight other boys and house mother Ellen Atim in their home for lunch. He sat quietly and was picking at his food. He suddenly developed a bad nosebleed. Mama Ellen brought him a cool cloth, but soon Joshua also began to spit up blood and she saw there was even bleeding from his ears. Blood actually got onto the tablecloth and on the clothes of the mom and children who were trying to help him.

"One of the children ran to get me, and Mother Ellen and I wrapped Joshua in a sheet and carried him to the office. I grabbed the keys to our director's car and Ellen and I drove him to the local hospital. Soon the entire sheet was soaking in blood, and our hearts were gripped with fear. I knew what these symptoms meant; a fatal and highly contagious bleeding disease like the dreaded Ebola or perhaps Marburg syndrome which had appeared in other areas of Uganda.

"My heart was filled with fear.

"I sat with him throughout the afternoon, praying and singing songs to comfort him. But no one else came, no medical help at all. There was no doctor in that hospital that day. Little Opio Joshua passed away at about 6 pm. The child who had awakened that morning to take part in a parade was gone by nightfall.

"I stayed at the hospital that night because I had to remain there until his body could be released the next day.

"Meanwhile, the District health official visited Otino Waa and declared a total lockdown and quarantine of the village and school for two weeks. No one could go in or out at Otino Waa. Yet an American physician who was serving in another village came and bravely scrubbed the areas of the house and the office where there were stains from the child's blood. The boys in Joshua's house were to remain inside. Officials from International

Health were summoned in their hazmat suits.

"The next morning, I wrapped the little body in a clean sheet and drove to his home village. As I left the hospital, I saw health officials arrive to burn the bed coverings and the mat where Joshua had lain. At the village, Joshua's few relatives stood weeping at a distance. A grave had been hurriedly prepared at the health officials' direction - this is the procedure that was always followed when an epidemic threatened. I could not allow myself to leave until little Joshua was placed in a simple wooden coffin and I had prayed over his grave.

"I could not drive to my home and possibly expose my wife and children. I returned to my office at the entrance of Otino Waa village and began to pray. And all across the school grounds and houses, I could hear voices lifted in prayer and in singing. They were all afraid.

"We did not know where the disease had started. We had purchased a young steer in town the day before and put it in a pasture behind one of the buildings. Had little Joshua ventured out to pet the animal through the wire fence? We didn't know for sure, but the steer was killed and buried as a precaution. Had infected rainwater perhaps carried the virus to the field? We began to boil all the drinking and cooking water even longer than normal.

"We really did not know how this had started. But we all knew where it might lead. The official warned that many deaths would likely follow. We heard that there had already been two other deaths in the nearby town of Lira.

"I had had to face fear many times in my life. Fear of the violent LRA soldiers who had roamed Northern Uganda for years, taking children prisoners to serve as child soldiers and murdering villagers. Fear in times of drought if there would be enough food for all of the boys and girls who counted on us. Fear when malaria weakened some of our children and staff. Fear for my own life at the hand of thieves and robbers. Time and time again we had seen the strong hand of the Lord's protection and salvation. But this was different. A plague like this was an invisible ghost of a disease that could reach out and possibly destroy the many needy children that we had worked for years to save.

"The next day we waited to see if any symptoms were appearing in anyone else at Otino Waa. There were none. The next day there were none. And the next day there were none. This miraculous answer to prayer went on for the full two weeks of the quarantine. When the health officials declared the quarantine to be lifted, they were astonished and thankful that their dire prediction of doom had come to nothing.

"The Lord's Spirit has covered us with His Grace," we told them. We had seen many healings at the Otino Waa village over the years. But my wife and I and Pastor Douglas and all the staff and orphans had never experienced anything as amazing as this, the protection from an epidemic. I suddenly was greatly encouraged that the Lord's hand was clearly on this ministry. In just a few weeks we would hold the upper level (high school) graduation for many of the first orphans who had first been taken in to save them from abduction by the rebel soldiers. These graduates would soon go on to become nurses and teachers and doctors and lawyers and even computer geniuses.

"The fact that this miracle happened the very week when our beloved founders were retiring and returning to their family in Oregon was a sign to us. It was a sign that God's plan for this place and these dear people would go forward and grow in the years to come. It was a sign for Bob and Carol that their work would endure."

The fourteen years Carol and I spent in Uganda were, without a doubt, the most challenging years of our lives. Living cross-culturally in a land with much poverty presented problems and situations completely outside our previous experiences. But those years were also the most productive! That kept us going back year after year. To have missed the Uganda chapter of our lives would have been a huge loss. We are so grateful that the Lord preserved us through all our struggles.

"He will be the sure foundation for all time, a rich storehouse of salvation and wisdom and knowledge."
- Isaiah 33:6

>> Epilogue
ONGOING IMPACT

The documentary film, "Lost & Found", produced by Sandy Cummings, tells the fascinating connection between Ugandan orphans and inmate artists in Oregon. Their artwork sales supports orphans

Bob & Carol, Sandy Cummings, and Milt Buehner at the My Hero awards ceremony.

halfway around the world. Lost and Found won a Hero Award from the 2012 University of Southern California My Hero International Film Festival. Learn more at https://myhero.com/film_lostfound and stream the full documentary on Apple TV.

In the years since our departure from full-time service in Uganda, so much has happened: Otino Waa has welcomed new American directors and is now led by Rev. Dickens. Hundreds of children have become adults, contributing to the health of their society. Additional programs have been added, more buildings have been built, and the mission continues forward.

Look at what PATH Ministries has reported in a recent year:
  - 779 children in our programs (including 60 in Ethiopia)
  - Four new water wells were drilled, serving thousands
  - Five new churches were planted
  - Over 9,000 people were served through our medical clinic, with 30 new babies born
  - The Otino Waa girls' soccer team went all the way to Nationals, finishing 6th in the nation.

"These are only some of the wonderful things that God has done [this year]. Perhaps the most beautiful highlights are much harder to measure - finding hope, dignity, confidence and a sense of belonging."

And the biggest change in my life, and why you're reading my words when Carol was always the better writer: my dear wife graduated to heaven. If you'd like to read more about her end of life journey and my ruminations on the glories of heaven with Carol there, read my Very Small Book, "Glimpses of Heaven."

>> Testimonies from Otino-Waa Orphans

Patrick Hamza

"I arrived at the Otino Waa Village on June 6, 2006. I was brought in as a very vulnerable child, and at that time I was in primary class two. When I reached Otino Waa, I was blessed by receiving a good education, and with the help of excellent teachers and encouragement, I began to believe that I could be a bright student. I also found the love of Jesus.

"Bob Higgins was the biggest inspiration to me in terms of how to think and how to find solutions to everyday problems. I remember clearly the day when he came to the weekly student's meeting to tell us that precious water was being wasted by many of us when taps were left running and unattended. He had noticed this during his daily walks around our circles of homes, and I remember feeling bad that I might be one of those being careless. But Bob brought up a practical solution; and several of us watched him as he installed taps that were designed in a new way which required manual pressure for any water to flow out. He was very inventive about solving the problems that arose from housing and feeding hundreds of children!

"Bob inspired me to use my brain to explore problems and think of answers. I believe this was what made me excited about the career path I chose in computing and robotics. Several of us senior students began to design our own small robots which won awards and we were eventually chosen to be on the Ugandan National Robotics Team. I was actually able to travel to Washington DC for the International competition! In the U.S. we competed against teams from over 160 countries. When the judging was over, we ranked third in all the nations of African, and 16th in the global competition.

"Today, I am the founder of Soilla AI, and the cofounder of Mwonyaa Streams and Kakebe technologies. We offer scientific and technical IT services and training throughout out nation. It is an amazing life for one who started as a vulnerable little boy who had no hope for a bright and useful future. All this was made possible by the faith and love of Bob and Carol Higgins."

Patricia Ameny
"My childhood was marked by the brutal war caused by the LRA rebels. The LRA attacked our village one night and killed both my parents, and I was kidnapped by the soldiers and taken far away. Eventually, I made it back to the home of my dear grandmother who was very poor, but she tried to care for me and my

siblings. Rev. Dickens heard of my situation and offered me a home at Otino Waa.

"When I arrived at Otino Waa, I began to heal from my years of trauma because Auntie Carol and Pastor Bob showed me so much love, and also I was with other orphans whose stories were like mine.. At our Ilera Community Church, I learned that God loved me and had a plan for my life, (Jeremiah 29:11) and I learned the joy of singing.

"Carol had four simple rules in class that shaped my character and also gave me confidence. They were "Speak Up", "Be Responsive", "Be Responsible", and "Follow Directions." I got the best quality education available to a child in Uganda and was able to get good scores on the national tests upon graduation.

"I joined the Good Samaritan School of Nursing and Midwifery (Lira) where I did a certificate course in midwifery. Later I was offered a place in the Verika School of Nursing at the hospital in Fort Portal where I worked and earned my Diploma as a Midwife. I am now waiting to join the medical University to become a gynecologist, intending to found a rural health clinic to help mothers and babies.

"I cannot put into words my thankfulness for Bob and Carol Higgins, for Pastor Dickens and all my teachers, for the house moms, and for my sponsors. My goal is to use my life to give back for all I have received."

Gabriel Obua

"I was not sure how old I was when I was given safety by Pastor Bob and Auntie Carol. I was the last born of six children, and my dear mother was illiterate so my birth was not recorded. She died when I was very young. At first, I was placed in the home of relatives, but soon I was taken to a small orphan home. Life there was very hard since we had barely one meal a day and no bedding or clean water. Despite that, I tried to get to school when I could. I was there beginning in 1999.

"Sometimes local pastors or missionaries came and took our pictures and gave us a few items, but they never came back. In around 2002 the Higgins came, and they were very concerned about how we were living. And they came back! They began bringing us items like buckets for water and towels and soap and blankets. They also began to send us food items like big sacks of rice and beans.

"In 2003 life became very dangerous because young people were being abducted all around us, and all we children could do was pray for we had no other safety. Then Rev. Dickens arrived to rescue us with a big truck sent by Bob and Carol, and they found a place for us to sleep in the Lira School for a time.   They hurried to build the first orphan homes on land they had purchased. My home had 8 boys and a house mom and even beds for each of us.

"Auntie Carol said I needed a birth date to go forward in schooling and she chose January 1 because it is easy to remember! As to the year of my birth, my siblings told me that it was in the time of the Karamojong Cattle Raiders when tribesmen from the north came to rustle our people's cattle. That was from 1986 to 1989, so

I have chosen 1986 as my birth year.

"Bob and Carol were the ones who tamed my wild nature. They taught us that even an orphan can succeed and find hope. I was beyond the grade levels that were taught in the first years of Otino Waa, but I was given vocational training personally by Carol and Bob, and soon I was managing the Otino Waa Tower Cafe and the Town Center Cafe. But I began to feel my calling was to serve my people in another way. So I studied very hard at night in my Otino Waa home until I was able to complete advanced level Senior 6.

"Then Bob and Carol encouraged me to sit for paper exams and when I passed (though barely) I was able to join the Law Development Center in 2012 where I received my ordinary diploma in law. In 2013 I joined Kampala International University to earn my Bachelor's Degree in Law. In 2017 I sat for my entry Bar Exam and that time I passed very well! I went on to earn my postgraduate Diploma in Legal Practice in 2018.

"In 2019 I was appointed as an Advocate of the High Court of Uganda, and all other courts in the nation are subordinate to that. It was an incredible honor but came with weighty responsibilities. In 2022 I went into private practice with PONSIANO OKELLO & CO ADVOCATES.

"The need to be most addressed is the issue of land ownership. People who were displaced in years of war or to refugee camps have to fight for their family land, and these cases end up in our courts. Also, there is the problem of people detained for years waiting for a proper trial.

"In 2020 I married my dear wife Brenda Obua. In loving Memory of what Carol did for me and so many, we have started a small medical facility near us named the Carol Memorial Medicare. I believe it will grow someday to help many. The Higgins and Rev. Dickens taught me what it means to be faithful to the work God sets before you, and I am forever grateful.for their guidance and for their example."

Edith Oruru Adong

"By the time I was 10 years old, I had lost both of my parents, and I was left to care for my two little sisters, Naomi and Serena. We were living in a tiny home left to us by our father in a town called Apec. It is very difficult to be the head of the family as a child, especially when that child was me. Times became so hard at this time that we could not afford to go to the government school where fees were very small. I cared for my sisters as best I could but I was filled with growing despair.

"Then on an amazing day, a wonderful man name Reverend Dickens came to meet us. He had heard about the plight of my two little sisters and had come to offer them a place at an orphan school named Otino Waa. It was not part of the plan for me to go because there was room in classes for the younger ones, and also I don't think Otino Waa had ever taken in three from one family before. But my little sisters and I were crying very hard at the thought of being separated and they were clinging to me. Rev. Dicken's heart was so moved that he loaded me into his vehicle also.

"I think it was a miracle from God that we all ended up at Otino Waa. We had a house with a Mom! We felt so loved. I didn't have to worry about food for the next day. We had rice and beans and greens that we cooked in our house of eight girls. And I did not have to worry that we would grow up uneducated. Education is everything in Uganda.

"We also got to go to the Ilera Community Church and learned singing and dancing with many friends. We also had a Creed that was written just for us and I learned that God loved me and had a plan for me. All these things changed my story because I had lost hope for my future when my mother and then my father passed.

"I lived and studied at Otino Waa for the next ten years and I received excellent help from the teachers and administrators and pastors and sponsors and even social workers.

When I passed my exams at Otino Waa, I went to study and received a Social Workers Certificate. By the grace of God, I am now pursuing a bachelor's degree in social work and social administration. I hope to be able to go serve the community of Odek where there are so many patients who suffer from the physical illness called the Nodding Syndrome.

"I don't have silver or gold or any way to repay dearest Carol and Bob for all they did for me, but I will do my best to do as they did and to change lives like my life was changed."

Janan Ogwang

"I lost my father in a road accident in 2005 when I was 10 years old. I have three brothers and two sisters- and I was the youngest. I could barely afford to attend any school. My mother was a peasant farmer scratching out an existence for us. But then this was also the time when the LRA rebels brought their violence and death to our area, Abia parish. We had to relocate to a refugee camp in the city.

"I was often out with an older brother just looking for food. But then a blessing came when an aunt, who was a primary teacher, offered to send my older brother to school. He later was able to complete a certificate in agriculture and to connect me with a wonderful man named Dickens Anyati who oversaw an orphan school.

"Rev. Dickens brought me to Otino Waa where I joined my new family and fellow students and my life changed forever. When I completed Primary 7, I tested number 4 in my entire group. When the Ointo Waa secondary school started I graduated with my upper-level certificate and went immediately to St. Elizabeth's Institute of Health Professionals in Kampala. That is where I graduated with a Medical Laboratory Technician.

"When I came back to Otino Waa the newly built clinic did not have a lab. Yet with the help of sponsors, we were able to get some equipment like a powerful microscope. From that day until now I still run our clinic. I can do diagnostic testing of blood smears for the four types of malarial parasites, and urine tests for things like fungal infections, gonorrhea, etc. I am now able to dispense many medicines from our pharmacy and also run vaccination clinics for mothers and babies.

"While I continue my work at Otino Waa, I also am completing a 3-year degree at the Lira Institute of Medical Technique. I am also blessed with my wife, Joy, and our two boys. My time at Otino Waa gave me not only an education but also taught me the ability to know how to be a good husband and father. Auntie Carol and Pastor Bob and Rev. Dickens and our teachers gave us so much compassion and this changed my heart. I thank God for their example and I pray that God will use me to help the disadvantaged.

"I always remember the words of our Creed; "Life may be hard, but God is Good all the time."

Sedrick Otolo

"In 2002, when I was just four years old, my father passed away leaving my young mother to care for three little boys. On the days when I could go to school, I was sad about the condition of our village's small school building. We had a few books and little supplies. I dreamed of getting to go to a real school. My prayer was answered on July 17, 2007, at 7:30 am when I was granted the opportunity to enter Otino Waa Children's Village. This turning point in my life occurred when I was nine years old.

"The encouragement I received from nurturing house mothers and teachers and the founders Bob and Carol Higgins made me feel welcome and embraced. We had the textbooks we needed and there was even a computer lab! And we had sports to help us grow strong, and time for fun with music and singing. The valuable lessons I learned from the Higgins, particularly the importance of speaking up and being responsive, shaped my character. As a result of that, I am now busy as an advocate for young people, teaching and guiding them across different sectors

"Under the motto of "Seize your moment," and inspired by that remarkable couple and Rev. Dickens, I worked hard in all my classes at Otino Waa. I did well in the national exams that are given to all Ugandan students at the end of each level. My interests were in the area of Communication Technology (ICT) and robotics. In 2018 I joined Isbat University to earn a Professional Certificate in Software Engineering and then earned a Diploma in Networking and Cyber Security. Currently, I am pursuing a Bachelor's Degree in Artificial Intelligence at the same university.

"In 2021 I was honored to receive the prestigious Uganda Innovation Award, where I had the privilege of shaking the hand of the President of Uganda. I wished that Auntie Carol and Pastor Bob had been there to see that day.

"I am a Co-founder of Kabeke Technologies Limited. My early life in the village led me to become the team leader in developing PREGCARE, a pregnancy monitoring device to help rural women.

"Like many of my fellow students at Otino Waa, I dared to go forward because we had been taught that God had a plan for our lives no matter how humble our beginnings were. I remembered the little books that Auntie Carol had written and illustrated for us, and it inspired me to write a book, "Being Victorious".

"Whenever I am asked to stand before young people as an inspirational speaker, I share the message of how faith and determination can transform an orphaned child into an impactful member of society. I owe this remarkable journey to the guidance and support of Bob and Carol Higgins and Rev Dickens. They taught us that our help comes from the Lord. And they were the vessels through which God directed my path. My heart overflows with gratitude."

Moses Apili

"I lost my mother to HIV when I was seven years old and one year later I also lost my father to that disease. Life became so hard for us eight siblings. My little sister Peninah and I were taken to a makeshift orphan home in Alito. The conditions there were very bad because of the surrounding fighting of the warlord Coney. The boys slept in one little room on a dirt floor and the girls in another. We had scraps of clothing and little food - sometimes we only had rice for one meal a day. Whenever we heard that the rebels were coming close to us, we hid in the bushes as the safest place to sleep.

"A kind pastor named Dickens Anyati and his friends Bob and Carol Higgins heard of our danger and one day sent a container truck to bring us to sleep in a school In Lira near land they had purchased to build Otino Waa.

"I was there to see the first brick buildings go up that would become the circle of houses that would become our true home.

They were so beautiful, and there was a strong fence around us to protect us. We had clothes to wear and 3 meals every day, and the Higgins got our schooling started right away. Besides classroom studies, we learned other practical skills. I was chosen to be part of the bee-keeping project and later I learned baking and was given a job at the Otino Waa cafe in Lira town.

My real dream was to become a driver for the school and students. Through the help of a sponsor, I was able to go to driving classes and pass all the exams and receive my license. I am thankful that this is now my ministry for Otino Waa. Ten years ago I married my wife Brenda and we have three healthy children and care for an orphan girl named Naomi.

"My dear sister Peninah has grown up to be a school teacher and she helps vulnerable children and orphans in her village. We were cast away as children in the time of war, but we were found and made whole by the Grace we found at Otino Waa village."

James Okori

"When I was a young boy, the number of orphans in the nation of Uganda was staggering. The brutality and killings by the LRA soldiers, the AIDS epidemic, the problem of famine and malnutrition, and other diseases like malaria and typhoid left many of us homeless.

"For a while, I lived with others like myself in a small location called an orphanage, but it was just a roof over our heads. We had little education because we could not afford the local school fees. Sometimes we went several days without food, and there was little sanitation and no medicine. The poor villagers around us could contribute little because they were also poverty-stricken.

"When I was accepted at Otino Waa, the major healing I needed was growing to understand what security and safety felt like. I learned what it was to sleep well. I was with others who also needed to heal. Dear Auntie Carol wrote what was called the Otino Waa Creed. We stood and recited this together every day, and soon we had memorized it. It gave us hope for our futures and taught us about the caring of the Lord.

"The quality of education there was very high. At night we studied around the table with the lights of kerosene lamps. We began to compete in class with other students — it was a friendly competition and camaraderie. I began even thinking of going on for further education, maybe something in the medical field.

"I was very interested in eye care because there are many sight problems in areas of poverty. I was able to enroll in studies for optometry. That is my field today. I am an ophthalmic clinical officer working at the Otino Waa clinic. I am thankful for having the use of a slit lamp - a microscope for examining eyes.

"What I owe to Bob and Carol and Rev. Dickens and the house mothers they provided for us is a debt I can't repay. I offer my prayers for them daily. I want to follow in their footsteps by giving services to orphans here and in this area. I have a wife and one child and three other children that I am taking care of. At Otino Waa, I learned what it was to be loved, and how to give love in return."

Gertrude Ajok

"I was privileged to graduate from Otino Waa in 2015. Being at Otino Waa was what taught me to love others because I had never understood love until I was brought there.

"I remember as a child being taken for treatment to the old clinic. Actually the original clinic was just a small room behind the school library . There were shelves of medicines that had been arranged by Auntie Carol; medicine for fevers and antibiotics and ointments for our wounds and all kinds of bandages. It was the first time in my life that I had received any medical help. No one had ever taken my temperature! I was overwhelmed by the feeling of being cared for. That very moment was when I new that I wanted to study medicine.

"Now, as an adult, I have become a nurse and I love this occupation. When someone is in pain and you are able to give them the help that they need, it is really incredible. And seeing a patient be healed is the best feeling in the world.

"I especially love helping the orphans here, and other community children. I can offer them the love and the physical , tangible care that impacted me so much when I was a child. Thanks be to Auntie Carol for her vision, and to all of those who gave for our new wonderful clinic with ultrasound machine and microscopes and even dental chairs! And my favorite addition - the birthing center where expecting mothers receive excellent care."

>> Acknowledgements

It was a great surprise to me that I was the one doing the writing of this book. For all of our married life, Carol had been the writer. She wrote well, with emotion, feeling, and descriptive detail. But she died of a brain tumor before the book could be written.

Friends Don Lang and Judy Renner reminded me that I was the only one who knew the whole story and I needed to start writing. Their urging convinced me to take pen and get chapter by chapter on paper. Much thanks to them for their gentle shove.

My long time friend Jim Tucker happened to be very good with English, and did the copy edit. He labored many hours correcting each chapter I sent his way. His fine tuning was an essential up-grade to everything I wrote.

Mari Hanes gave her perceptive overview of the book in general as story editor. Some chapters were renamed, chapter order was switched around, some chapters were rewritten for clarity or enhanced interest. The book would not be what it is now without her skillful touches.

Brent Earwicker turned the chapters into a book. He formatted the print to fit the page, added the pictures, placed each book section in its proper place. He labored through several edits to get all the details just right. I am so grateful!

And a special thanks to the many people who served on the board over the years. The team effort brought progress in dealing with many facets of the international ministry.

Read more from Bob Higgins at his blog:
https://medium.com/@robertjhiggins

Learn more about Otino Waa Children's Village and the ongoing work of PATH International at *https://pathinternational.co*

www.ingramcontent.com/pod-product-compliance
Lightning Source LLC
LaVergne TN
LVHW041329190125
801587LV00001B/2